AGAINS

AGAINST ESTABLISHMENT

An Anglican Polemic

Theo Hobson

DARTON · LONGMAN + TODD

First published in 2003 by
Darton, Longman and Todd Ltd
1 Spencer Court
140–142 Wandsworth High Street
London
SW18 4JJ

The right of Theo Hobson to be identified as the author
of this work has been asserted in accordance with the
Copyright, Designs and Patent Act 1988.

ISBN 0 232 52508 0

A catalogue record for this book is available from the British Library.

Designed by Sandie Boccacci
Phototypeset in 11.25/12.75pt Perpetua
by Intype Libra Ltd
Printed and bound in Great Britain by
Cox and Wyman Ltd, Reading

For Tess and Martha,
who support me

Love is not one of the duties that we owe to the state.

Karl Barth, *Church and State*, 1939

As the philosopher Nietzsche says, 'What does not kill you makes you stronger.'

Rowan Williams (on being asked if disestablishment would destroy the Church, February 2002)

Contents

Preface

⟊━➤━⟊

THIS BOOK IS INTENDED as a provocative essay rather than an authoritative study. Its treatment of a hugely complex issue is manifestly incomplete, and sometimes rather cavalier. In my defence, I would say that the issue is so important (though you would not know it from most Anglican theology) that there is room for all sorts of approaches to it, even this. Thanks to Brendan Walsh of DLT for backing it.

Introduction

†══════†

LET ME GUESS what you think about the establishment of the Church of England. You think some changes are probably necessary: if the Church is to regain cultural respect it must not seem to be subservient to the state, or unfairly privileged. But you are wary of calls for disestablishment: the old arrangement still underpins the identity of both Church and nation and cannot be lightly tossed aside. In other words, you want to see a dynamic, autonomous Church that retains its national role. In other words, you want to have your cake and eat it.

The idea of national religious unity is no longer a feasible narrative. It was never strictly true, of course, but for the vast majority it once had the aura of truth: it worked. No longer. It now fosters cynicism and impedes cultural renewal. But this is a merely secular concern. It is when we begin to speak in religious terms that things become serious. The Church of England, by its very nature, associates the Gospel of Jesus Christ with a sixteenth-century ideal of national unity.

Establishment gives the Church of England an image problem that is way off the scale. It is like a young man at a disco, on the pull. Though he is handsome and a good dancer, his attempts at courtship consistently fail. Could his difficulty be related to the surprising fact that he is shackled to his grandmother? This Church is tied to an obsolete social ideology; to a vague sacralisation of the nation and the monarch. Is it any surprise that young, intelligent people react to this institution with a distaste that is tinged with pity? Let us try to see afresh the contemporary poverty of this tradition; its alienation from the cultural and intellectual life of the nation. Contemporary Anglican sensibility is a choice of decadence. Over here we have the traditionalist, a ruddy pedant, angry about women. And over here is the Evangelical, who displays a very different sort of decadence: a shocking anti-intellectualism, a scary sentimentality. Yes, there are liberal Anglicans too, but generally speaking they lack all conviction.

My thesis obviously relates to questions of 'national identity'. Freud's greatest insight, which redeems all his nonsense, is that health depends upon honesty. It applies to the body politic also. The disestablishment of the Church does not entail a cultural revolution. It entails being honest about a cultural revolution that has already taken place. Over the past generation or so, Britain has rejected its traditional religious identity. This should be seen as the completion of a much longer process of secularisation, of course. Its gradual nature threatens to obscure its import. This rejection of the Church by the national political culture amounts to a revolution, perhaps the biggest in our history. Yet the outward forms remain in place. It is an odd situation, and rather an unhealthy one. Consequently, to argue against establishment is like trying to kill a ghost. It is a rather embarrassing undertaking.

How has establishment lasted so long, if it is anomalous on two counts – modern secular politics and Christian theology? Principally due to the cultural conservatism of the majority, of course. But why has the Church itself agreed to remain within such a theologically dubious arrangement? Principally because it shares this cultural conservatism. Also, the abandonment of status is a bitter thing: it is hard to climb down from such a high pedestal. And of course we must refer to the Church's famous internal schism between Catholic and Protestant, or 'high' and 'low', the depth and bitterness of which can hardly be overstated. One of its effects is to make each side institutionally conservative, for fear of ceding influence to the other side.

But something more must be said about the internal rift. In a sense it is the real concern of this book: without close reference to it, 'disestablishment' is an empty slogan, mere journalistic bluster. This Church has been defined by its pursuit of the 'middle way', or *via media*, between Catholic and Protestant; it has attempted to hold together the warring principles of Western Christianity. And to a remarkable extent it has done so: an incredible achievement, the ecclesiological equivalent of getting the lion and the lamb to chum up. But this achievement is unthinkable without the Church's establishment: an overarching political ideal was needed, to make the fragile union work. Recently, the unifying force of establishment has greatly weakened, and the middle way with it. In the last decade or two, the Church has failed to keep its extremist edges in check – the centre cannot hold. We now have the worst of both worlds: open schism within an unpopular established Church. What is to be done? We cannot revive the middle way, because it is dependent on establishment, a dying idea. In the mid nineteenth century, as we shall see, it was possible to overcome schism through renewed emphasis on the Church's national role; no longer.

So what is to be done? We need to reinvent the middle way, away from establishment; forge a new basis for it. I am not pretending that this is a straightforward process, but one thing seems certain: we must be ready to let go of what is comfortable and habitual. We must clear away the old, to make room for the new.

An example of the old Anglican approach: in March 2003 a Church newspaper offered a brief profile of a new bishop-designate: 'Canon Oliver dislikes labels, enjoying both the dignity and theatre of high church worship and the warmth and excitement of evangelical and charismatic worship.'[1] How nice. But what if the vocation of this Church is not to affirm both of these forms (which flourish elsewhere without its help), but to expose their inadequacy? The middle way needs a sharper sense of purpose; it needs definition, teeth. This is my sub-plot.

Most of my argument takes historical form: Chapter One is concerned with the recent history of the Church of England, the years of the present Queen's reign, especially the most recent years. Chapter Two takes a step back and offers an account of the history of establishment since the Reformation. Chapter Three engages with various twentieth-century defences of establishment, and then looks at Rowan Williams' rather ambiguous stance.

I had intended to add a final chapter sketching out the positive theological basis for my position. I have opted to leave that for another time. Another omission might as well be acknowledged: this book offers no systematic typology of Church–state relations, and no theoretical definitions of 'establishment' and 'Church'. And another: it passes over the constitutional and ecclesiastical technicalities surrounding the prospect of disestablishment, which are manifold and rather tedious (who would own Westminster Abbey? etc.). But perhaps the latter omission is intentional. To pay too much attention to the legal-constitutional complexity is to miss the forest for the twigs. For example, certain commentators have recently said an amazingly stupid thing about disestablishment. They have said that it would be 'too complicated'; a minefield, a drain on parliamentary and synodical time. It is difficult to know how to react to this. Christianity has always been too complicated, especially in its transitional stages: let us take it for granted that its coming renewal will be also. The aim of this book is to suggest why such complexity is inescapable.

Essentially I am offering a critique of the Church of England. Here is the nub of it: this Church is locked in a terrible, terminal dilemma. It has always depended on establishment for its unity, its coherence, its order, its *identity*. But establishment is gradually draining it of vitality, of credibility. For it is increasingly obvious that the traditional national ideal is at best irrelevant, and at worst inimical, to the business of Christianity. A convincing and compelling form of Christianity cannot afford to be defined in this way.

In consequence, Anglican identity has become intolerably painful. To be an Anglican is to be in some degree of denial (or ignorance) about this crisis. Surely, with some tinkering, the circle can be squared? Surely the constitution will evolve in some unforseeable way and the problem will recede? Surely a new leader will show the way? Another habit is to affect a brave realism, almost an indifference. Let disestablishment come if it must: the Church will survive! And in the meantime let us carry on doing what we do, being what we are! But this is to evade the immediacy and the finality of the crisis. We would do better to acknowledge the unpalatable truth. This Church, as it is presently constituted, is a sinking ship. We must work hard to rescue the priceless cargo, to man the lifeboats. And all the while we are told to keep everything shipshape and, bitter irony, to get others on board.

Should polemicists ever admit to misgivings? My theological sympathies are largely liberal. I am no admirer of fundamentalism. I would not join a church that wasn't rich in tolerance, humour, moral equivocation. The Church of England has these virtues, more than any other religious institution ever. And disestablishment would endanger them. Yes, it would also jeopardise the fragile unity of this Church. Most advocates of disestablishment promise that the Church would emerge stronger and more united, as if they're advising a company to reposition itself in the market on the basis of reliable data. Let us be a little more honest. The Church would be leaping into the unknown, dying to itself, living by *faith*.

Finally let me venture a note of humility. The institution that I attack in these pages, often rather sarcastically, has been upbuilt by many great and selfless witnesses to the Gospel. May they forgive this itchy rant from a young man in a hurry.

Chapter One

※━━━※

UNDEAD:

ESTABLISHMENT SINCE 1953

TRADITIONALLY, ESTABLISHMENT was a two-way deal: the Church gave spiritual legitimacy to the state, and the state promoted the interests of the Church. During the twentieth century, especially since the 1960s, the state effectively pulled out of this arrangement, by popular demand. The nation became effectively secular. The Church ought to have acknowledged this new reality, and started to redefine its role. Instead it chose to pretend that nothing had really changed. It overlooked the state's abandonment of the age-old deal. From one perspective, it began to resemble a wife who accepts her husband's infidelity, who prefers a sham marriage to no marriage at all. It is a rather pathetic tale.

One historian comments, 'The religious history of England in the twentieth century may well be character-ised as one of a steadily growing separation between Church and society.'[1] Such a separation, of course, is no friend to establishment. For establishment is rooted in an identification of Church and society, in the idea that they are ultimately the same thing. At the start of the twentieth century this idea was paid lip service but lacked real credibility. Thanks to Darwin and Huxley, Marx and Morris, Hardy and Yeats, the English intelligentsia was largely secularised before the First World War. The most respected writers and thinkers were agnostics or atheists: religious believers were slightly shocking exceptions (Woolf saw Eliot's faith as a sort of betrayal). The trend has continued ever since, of course, despite a partial religious reaction in the 1940s. The cultural rejection of religion is one of the most obvious narratives of twentieth-century Britain.

But the Anglican order was slow to totter. A significant bulwark was the Church's role in the educational establishment. Another factor was the justified fear of political change: like the French Revolution before it, the Russian Revolution, with its anarchy and tyranny, made traditional structures, however lacking in credibility, seem rather sensible. Despite the gradual drift towards secularism, the national mood remained one of cultural conservatism during the first half of the twentieth century. Consequently, the Church suffered from a false sense of security. The two world wars added to this paradoxical situation, in which the Church's position seemed to be far more secure than it was. Each war secured short-term popularity for the Church, but earned it the suspicion of the next generation.

In the early 1950s the Church seemed, from a distance, to have weathered the storms of the century. The Coronation of 1953 seemed to be a moment of vindication and renewal for the established Church, and for the nation as a whole. In defiance of the spirit of the age, it seemed that Britain could find succour in ancient religious verities. In reality the spirit of the age was not so easily defied. The 1950s was really the last gasp of our national religious myth, and in 1953 the illusion of stability was most complete.

In a sense, Churchill is the key figure in understanding the spirit of the Coronation, not the Archbishop of Canterbury or the Queen. He was far keener on monarchy than on Christianity; he reacted to it with histrionic chivalry, like some hoary knight. Indeed he was knighted shortly before the Coronation, which 'added to the sense of the great statesman as secular high priest of the coming ceremony'.[2] On the Queen's accession he called the monarchy 'the magic link which unites our loosely bound, but strongly interwoven commonwealth'. He rejoiced that 'God save the Queen' would return to use – singing it was surely his most heartfelt expression of Anglican faith.

The coronation of a monarch is the ultimate symbol of the Church of England's involvement in the state, and the state's involvement in the Church. Coronations, in English history, are principally religious rather than constitutional ceremonies – which is why a long delay after accession is acceptable. The theology is decisively Old Testament (where it is not frankly pagan). Indeed, Handel's music in the service contains explicit reference to the anointing of Solomon.

In the spring of 1953, expectation welled up; shop windows began to display imitation regalia, and the popular press was full of royalist treacle. For the first time, the entire nation could participate in a royal event by means of television: in the run-up to Coronation day, the number of licence-holders doubled from 1.5 million to 3 million. The press practically gave up reporting other news; it pored over every detail of the coming ceremony. This meant that the Archbishop of Canterbury was suddenly a familiar face. Geoffrey Fisher 'took his own role in the proceedings with great seriousness, becoming – during the months in which anybody remotely connected with the drama acquired a celebrity status – one of the Coronation's most familiar actors'.[3]

Fisher had been appointed by Churchill in 1945, to replace the charismatic William Temple. Churchill had no interest in Church politics, but knew that this appointment mattered. The other contender was the outspoken Bishop Bell of Chichester, who dared to criticise Allied bombing policy. The choice of Fisher over Bell was clear evidence that Erastianism was alive and well. According to the theologian Donald MacKinnon, the passing over of Bell was a more serious blow for the Church than the death of Temple.[1] (Mrs Thatcher would later emulate her hero's habit of blocking 'wet' bishops from top jobs.)

Fisher typified Anglican conservatism. Aged just 27, he had succeeded Temple as headmaster of Repton, a public school. This career path, from headmaster to bishop, was fairly normal. The Church was more or less like a huge public school, or rather it was the chapel of the national school. An archbishop was not expected to be much of a theologian, just as a head boy isn't expected to be awfully bright. Incidentally, while a headmaster Fisher had taught the author Roald Dahl. He later recounted that Fisher had administered such severe beatings that Dahl was put off Christianity for life. He was also a Mason. Adrian Hastings writes: 'He lacked charisma, theology or ideology. "Commonsense" was his favourite expression and the source of his wisdom . . . His considerable intellectual powers he exercised chiefly upon *The Times* crossword.'[5]

Before the event, the Archbishop reflected on its meaning. The Queen was 'God-called'. The monarchy's reduced political role did not reduce her national significance: it gave her 'the possibility of a spiritual power far more exalted and far more searching in its demands: the power to lead, to inspire, to unite, by the Sovereign's personal character, personal convictions, personal example'. She would be a beacon of 'domestic fidelity' and 'united homes'.[6] He also stressed the sacrificial element; that she was bearing this burden for the sake of others. Fisher thus made explicit what the symbolism suggested. The Church was making full use of the cult of personality; it looked to this young woman as a sort of walking sacrament.

The nation was never happier with its Church. Instead of gloomy abstract religion, it was cooking up a real-life holy spectacle, like something out of *Snow White*. Royal personality cult suffused with vague religiosity is obviously the ideal religion of the English people: Diana's funeral provides more recent evidence. And intelligent culture colludes. Thus *The Times* on Coronation Day declared that:

> every man and woman in the land [is] a partaker in the mystery of the Queen's anointing. But also the Queen stands for the soul as well as the body of the Commonwealth. In her is incarnate on her Coronation day the whole of society, of which the state is no more than a political manifestation. She represents the life of her people . . . as men and women, and not in their limited capacity as Lords and Commons and electors.

It is worth briefly recalling what happened on 2 June 1953. The Queen entered Westminster Abbey in a crimson robe, symbolic of her sacrificial role. She made promises to govern properly, including a commitment to maintain 'the laws of God and the true profession of the Gospel, maintain the Protestant Reformed Religion established by law and maintain and preserve inviolably the settlement of the Church of England, and the doctrine, worship, discipline and government thereof, as by law established in England.' She said this with her right hand on a Bible, kneeling at the altar.

The anointing was done out of public view, while the choir sang the famous anthem 'Zadok the Priest and Nathan the Prophet'. She shed her robes and regalia and wore a simple white dress. Ben Pimlott writes: 'People were moved by the divestment, by the sense of exposure, and by the simplicity of the anointing dress – as though the sacrifice were a physical one, and the rite performed under the canopy an act of violation.'[7] In a prayer, the Archbishop compared this anointing to that of Jesus Christ. Before she was crowned, the Queen was 'invested' with certain pieces of jewellery and clothing, as if she was being ordained priest or bishop. Once he had crowned her, the Archbishop led the bishops and peers in paying homage to her, which meant acknowledging her superior spiritual authority. Ever since Henry VIII, the monarch had taken on certain characteristics of the ousted pope: this is the clearest enactment of the fact.

From a political perspective, the Coronation was a reassertion of the Tory vision. It said that nothing had really changed since the first Elizabeth. Now, as then, the nation's loyalty to the Queen and her Church remained the basis of politics. In an age of mass democracy, this was patently unrealistic, but the nation suspended disbelief. From one perspective this was surprising. Although the war had sharpened national identity, it had also brought a new era of democratic feeling. Churchill was voted out of office in 1945 and the welfare state was set up – a huge victory for the modernising Left. The national mood was fraught with contradiction. The welfare state itself reflects this: though it was radically modern, it was also a reassertion of traditional national identity. The 1950s saw a sort of cross-party alliance in favour of national unity, partly because the Left did not want to jeopardise its recent domination of the economic agenda by seeming unpatriotic. But in reality it was impatient for a more secular future. Adrian Hastings comments: 'The party of Gaitskell, Bevan, Wilson, Crosland, Crossman and Jenkins was a party to which matters of religious belief seemed oddly remote and in which "theology" came to be used to describe the meaningless, or the unnecessarily complicated.'[8]

The 1950s saw the restoration of a huge number of bombed churches. This reflected a less concrete reality – the attempted restoration of an old ideal of England. Fisher and his bishops set about reforming Canon Law, which many saw as a matter of irrelevance. But a rather sleepy view of old England dominated, and the Church was happy to comply. Hastings writes: 'Perhaps without too great absurdity one might suggest that the most suitable clerically produced literature of this undramatic age was that of the Revd Wilbert Vere Awdry, author of the *Railway Series*, a long and immensely popular set of children's books about talking engines, such as *Tank Engine Thomas* (1949), or *Gordon the Big Engine* (1953).'[9]

The Church was strongly represented in Parliament. The Conservative government was almost entirely made up of sincere Anglicans, of whom Enoch Powell was the most vociferous. The Tory spirit dominated the decade in cultural terms also. The writings of T. S. Eliot and C. S. Lewis were hugely influential.

But, of course, on closer inspection things looked less rosy for Christian Britain. A new secular intelligentsia was gaining confidence, and it could claim to have history on its side: statistics suggested that popular religion was on the wane. A survey in 1947 had found that 'religion . . . has in the minds of the great majority, become simply irrelevant to the question of living. It seems to have no connection with life and no relation to the real day-to-day problems of modern society.'[10] During the war, George Orwell had made a similar observation:

> Only about ten per cent of [the English people] ever go near a place of worship except to be married and buried. A vague theism and an intermittent belief in life after death are probably fairly widespread, but the main Christian doctrines have been largely forgotten. Asked what he meant by 'Christianity', the average man would define it wholly in ethical terms ('unselfishness', or 'loving your neighbour', would be the kind of definition he would give).[11]

In the early 1950s, Orwell's statistic remained broadly accurate, under the veneer of high traditionalism.

And, of course, the Church itself was not quite the traditionalist bastion of public perception. There were various radical stirrings in the Church during the 1950s, though they generally came to the surface in the following decade. The worldwide Anglican Communion had begun to exert a radicalising influence. It gave rise to the pioneering aid agency and pressure group Christian Action in 1945, which often took a different view of international affairs from the Foreign Office. For example, the Church acquired a vivid perspective on the situation in South

Africa through such priests as Trevor Huddleston, who toured Britain in 1956 stirring up indignation against apartheid. (Race was becoming an important domestic issue also, following the mass immigration from the Caribbean. The Church was shamefully slow to take a lead. As Stephen Sykes comments, Anglicans 'failed to make them welcome and to foster their contribution to the Church's life.')[12] In 1956 the Church was split over Suez, with Fisher himself one of those opposed to Eden's invasion of Egypt. Many Tories were annoyed by the Church's disloyalty: a sign of things to come. The next year Britain acquired her own hydrogen bomb: the Church was again split, and many clergy joined the Aldermaston March. In the new international situation, a Church strictly loyal to British foreign policy seemed unlikely.

The religious unity of the Church was also showing signs of strain. This was a result of separate religious revivals within each wing of the Church. The Evangelical wing was radicalised by Billy Graham's missions to the UK in 1954 and 1955. Graham's style was muted by the involvement of a high proportion of public-school types, led by John Stott, but it still seemed to many an intolerably un-English form of Christianity. Fisher said, in private, that its triumph in the Church 'would be an absolute disaster'; like countless of his predecessors, he warned against 'enthusiasm'.[13] Another critic was Michael Ramsey, the future Archbishop of Canterbury: he openly attacked the new-style evangelism as heretical and sectarian. Ramsey was a leading figure in the other revival that was under way, the Anglo-Catholic revival. It was connected to the Parish and People Movement, formed in 1949, that sought to put the Eucharist at the heart of parish life, and more widely to foster respect for the

Church as a sacramental community. During the 1950s, then, the Church was seeing a revival of interest in religious identity, from both of its wings. The united national Church of the Coronation was beginning to reveal the presence of two competing religious sub-cultures.

From a distance, however, the Church was strong and united, and its pervasive influence upon society was taken for granted. This influence naturally threw up anomalies, hypocrisies and conundrums. The cost was felt by one person in particular. Not long after her sister's accession, Princess Margaret fell in love with Group-Captain Peter Townsend, who was a divorcee. This was still a significant social stigma: it was beneath the dignity of royalty to be seen with divorcees, let alone marry them. And the Church had an interest in keeping this taboo alive: it opposed reform of the strict divorce law. This was a good example of the Church upholding an aspect of social morality that had lost real credibility. The Prime Minister, Anthony Eden, was himself divorced.

In 1955 feverish speculation surrounded the Princess's love life. On 31 October, under some degree of pressure from Fisher, she issued a statement in which she declared herself 'mindful of the Church's teaching that Christian marriage is indissoluble, and conscious of my duty to the Commonwealth'. Some wondered why a divorced prime minister should be allowed to appoint archbishops, yet a princess, highly unlikely to succeed to the throne, should not be allowed to marry her divorced lover. Soon Fisher sent a further message that the Church was opposed to the liberalisation of divorce: he championed an Act of Convocation in 1957 banning the remarriage of divorcees in church (it was repealed in 2002). Yet the Princess's renunciation soon seemed to belong to a distant world.

Peter Hitchens writes: 'Her gesture was too late. The fortress she sacrificed herself to defend had already fallen. In time, she would find that the rest of the country laughed at her rather than followed her good example.'[14]

One of Fisher's last public roles was as chief supporter of the 1960 prosecution of Penguin for its publication of an uncensored edition of *Lady Chatterley's Lover*. Clifford Longley comments: 'Why keeping the f-word out of the vocabulary of English literature was such a high priority for the Church of England can only be explained if the established church felt itself to be responsible for the entire moral tone of the country, and not just for the religious beliefs of its members.'[15] The 1960s began in 1961, once Fisher was off the scene. 'Archbishop Fisher was, perhaps, the last representative of the old order',[16] writes Adrian Hastings.

The revolution

Britian's transformation into a secular nation most obviously occurred during the 1960s. The liberal legislation that marks the transition had its roots in 1957, in the government's Report on Homosexual Offences and Prostitution, also known as the Wolfenden Report. The law existed 'to protect the public from harm', said the report, not to preach at them:

> It is not, in our view, the function of the law to intervene in the private lives of citizens, or to seek to enforce any particular pattern of behaviour . . . Unless a deliberate attempt is made by society . . . to equate the sphere of crime with that of sin, there must remain a realm of private morality and

immorality which is, in crude terms, not the law's business.[17]

The first piece of legislation to reflect the report was the Suicide Act of 1960, which decriminalised the deed.

In 1964 Harold Wilson came to power, and his Home Secretary Roy Jenkins implemented a series of reforms, beginning with the abolition of the death penalty. In 1968 abortions and homosexuality became legal. In 1969 the Divorce Reform Act was passed.

Obviously the Church was split on the wisdom of all these reforms. But this was a significant advance on Fisher's blanket conservatism. The Church was beginning to liberalise its official public voice. For example, three years before the divorce reform was passed, a Church committee had advised in favour: 'it is right and proper for the Church to cooperate with the state . . . in trying to make the divorce law as equitable and as little harmful to society as it can be made'.[18] But of course the Church did not change its teaching on the indissolubility of marriage; it was simply being realistic about the conduct of the undevout masses. Similarly, it continued to condemn homosexuality despite approving its decriminalisation. Ramsey told the Lords that he found homosexuality disgusting but that he also found its persecution inhumane. The Church was therefore learning, through necessity, to separate Christian morality from the law of the land – a separation which had never been necessary during the centuries of Christendom. It is not surprising that the sundering of social *mores* and Church teaching should produce decades of Christian trauma, and indeed a crisis of national identity. The survival of establishment has covered up, and so perpetuated, this trauma, this crisis.

The secularisation of culture in this period takes many other forms. In 1958, the government had moved Church schools into state control, which began the gradual weakening of their religious character. In higher education, a secular spirit was triumphant. The social sciences came to dominate the humanities; classics and philosophy, which had been conducive to theology, were seen as rather irrelevant. The whole ethos of the new universities was secular: the chaplain was not part of the institutional furniture, as he was in Oxbridge colleges. As a new novelistic genre attested, the university campus became the essentially secular space.

One of the most important spheres of secularisation was broadcasting. During the war the BBC had been explicitly involved in Christian propaganda, and this continued in a more muted form after the war. Sir William Haley declared in 1948 that 'the BBC . . . bases its policy on a positive attitude towards Christian values . . . The whole preponderant weight of its programmes is directed to this end.'[19] On Sundays three services were broadcast, plus other religious programmes. It was a controversial event when an agnostic or atheist expressed their views on air. There were howls of protest in 1955 when an academic called Margaret Knight gave a series of humanist talks; the BBC was accused of anti-Christian propaganda. Opinion polls supported this loyalty to 'Christian culture', as a key ingredient of national unity. The Methodist Donald Soper pointed out that 'Christians would do themselves harm if they assumed that the Christian faith was a hot-house plant which needed to be protected against all weathers.'[20] But this was considered radical: the Church was not used to the idea of cultural freedom.

The revolution of the 1960s is perhaps best summarised in relation to the notion of 'public decency'. In 1963 the Profumo Affair revealed two shocking facts that are now commonplace: even politicians have illicit sex, and millions of people are hungry to know every dirty detail. To many, Britain suddenly seemed a more sleazy place. Mary Whitehouse, a Midlands schoolteacher and Evangelical Christian, was one of them. In 1964 she launched her Clean-Up TV Campaign.

The Church was now led by Michael Ramsey, whose liberal Anglo-Catholicism was as intelligent and influential as that of the present Archbishop of Canterbury. In relation to establishment, as to most things, he was a liberal reformer. At his enthronement sermon he restated the Church's commitment to serve the national community: 'But in that service, and in rendering to God the things that are God's, we ask for a greater freedom in ordering and in the urgent revising of our forms of worship.'[21] It was the continuation of a campaign for greater autonomy that Temple had begun forty years earlier. Both men made it clear that such autonomy was for the sake of the Church's mission to the nation, rather than a means to disestablishment. Thirteen years later, Ramsey's demand was largely met, as we shall see.

In the early 1960s the nation was shocked to find that the Church contained people called theologians who questioned its teaching. In 1963 *Honest to God* by John Robinson, Bishop of Woolwich, was serialised in a Sunday paper. Part of Robinson's thesis was that traditional Christian morality must be replaced by a 'new morality' that emphasized compassion above all. This drew much traditionalist fire, but on one level it was simply a recognition of reality. When society liberalised, it was inevitable that an established Church would reflect this and show its most liberal face to the world. But many saw things the other way round, and blamed the Church's liberalisation for social problems, and even sensational crimes like the Moors murders. To blame liberal bishops for all this was irrational but understandable: they were sharp reminders of a lost order.

Robinson's type of theological radicalism was echoed over the next two decades, culminating in David Jenkins, Bishop of Durham, and Don Cupitt, who became famous with *Taking Leave of God* (1980). It was in general a very Ivory Tower sort of radicalism, very brave about Spinoza and Kant, but rather shy about political considerations. In particular it evaded questions about the Church's political situation: 'It might take leave of God but not of well-endowed canonries or deaneries', comments Adrian Hastings.[22]

During the sixties the decline in church attendance went into freefall. The decline had begun earlier in the century, but it had been very gradual indeed. The mid sixties were the real turning point. In 1960, for example, there were not substantially fewer Anglican baptisms than there had been in 1895 (the drop was from 64 per cent to 55). In 1970 the figure dropped to 46 per cent, which meant the rate of decline was now six times faster. The decline was reflected in the closure of churches and theological colleges. By 1968 there were 20 per cent fewer ordinands than the number of places available. A recent study of Britain's secularisation puts it starkly:

For a thousand years, Christianity penetrated deeply

into the lives of the people, enduring Reformation, Enlightenment and industrial revolution by adapting to each new social and cultural context that arose. Then, really quite suddenly in 1963, something very profound ruptured the character of the nation and its people, sending organised Christianity on a downward spiral to the margins of social significance.[23]

The impact of the permissive revolution on the function of the established Church cannot be overstated. To put it bluntly, it emptied establishment of cultural significance. Before the 1960s, Church and state had been united in their social conservatism. The teaching of the Church was to a large extent reflected in the law, and the law found some of its legitimacy in the backing of the Church. Of course, this was a weak version of a homogenous religious society, but that really was the model. In the 1960s, a revolution occurred. The state withdrew from its role as authoriser of moral practice. This meant that the Church's traditional role as authoriser of moral practice was also at an end, whether it liked it or not. No longer was there an official morality, backed by Church and state. Callum Brown writes:

> The complex web of legally and socially accepted rules which governed individual identity in Christian Britain until the 1950s has been swept aside since the 1960s. Secularisation is to be located, in part at least, in the changing conditions which allowed previously regarded Christian and social 'sins' to be regarded as acceptable and moral, at least by many, in British society in 2000.[24]

In November 1970 the new General Synod met for the

first time. It was a significant step in the direction of autonomy, and away from the old Erastian ideal. It replaced the Church Assembly, which had been created in 1919, and like its predecessor was composed of three houses: Bishops, Clergy and Laity. As Hastings comments, 'The Church would now be permitted, very largely, to rule itself, both because that is what it wanted to do and because the political establishment no longer bothered very seriously about this section of its former empire.'[25]

In the same year the Chadwick Report on Church–State Relations argued that the Church would benefit from greater autonomy, but that this need not mean disestablishment. In line with the thought of Temple and Ramsey, the aim was to loosen establishment, in order to help the Church to modernise its national role. It recommended that Synod, not Parliament, should become the final authority on matters of worship and doctrine, and that bishops should be selected by a specially established Church Committee. (Ramsey cared much more about the former than the latter reform.)

In 1974 Synod voted in favour of both of Chadwick's recommendations: that the Church should control its own worship and doctrine and that it should appoint bishops. Parliament accepted a compromised version of both of these demands. Worship and doctrine was almost entirely entrusted to the Synod, though it was not given a free hand over the Book of Common Prayer. And a compromise was reached on the appointment of bishops: the present system, in which the Crown Appointments Commission sends two names to the prime minister, who has the final say.

So two Erastian pillars were weakened but left in place during the 1970s. And there was careful avoidance of the larger question of whether the principle of a national Church was any longer worth defending. It was generally assumed to be so, despite the decline in Anglican allegiance. Declining church attendance tends to make Anglicans more defensive about establishment. If the masses do not get religion directly on Sundays, the thinking goes, it is even more important that they should receive it by the social osmosis of a 'Christian culture'. And so far it has always been possible to show that the majority are in favour of 'Christian culture' – just as they are in favour of the royal family and hanging.

Considered as part of the national furniture, the Church was popular enough. Yet considered in itself, the national religion was beginning to look embarrassingly weak. In 1975 the new Archbishop of Canterbury, Donald Coggan, launched the Call to the Nation which was about as successful as the more recent Decade of Evangelism. While Coggan admitted that there was no simple answer to the nation's problems, he helpfully noted that 'unless there is a concentrated effort to lift our whole national debate up into the moral sphere . . . we shall never find the answer'.[26] The Church seemed to hanker for a simpler age in which 'the moral sphere' was easier to define. Coggan laid particular emphasis on marriage; he asked that a Minister for the Family be appointed to this end. But the attempt to use the state to bolster 'Christian morality' was misguided; it made the Church seem reactionary, hungry for its former cultural power.

The sharp decline in church attendance continued. The statistical disaster of the 1960s was repeated in the 1970s. Indeed, the seventies were even worse – 80,000 worshippers were lost each year, and hundreds of churches were declared redundant (over a thousand between 1969 and

1984). 'It is not exaggerated to conclude that between 1960 and 1985 the Church of England as a going concern was effectively reduced to not much more than half its previous size', writes Paul A. Welsby.[27] One result of this was that the established Church had lost its overwhelming dominance of the religious marketplace. Whereas Catholic priests had recently been a small fraction of those working in Britain, their numbers now reached around half of the total Anglican presence. In urban areas, Catholic attendance was significantly higher than Anglican. But the Church's rural presence also diminished during the 1970s – livings were amalgamated, secondary institutions such as Sunday schools were in decline, and in many cases the local vicar had lost his social standing, his air of centrality. 'The majority of the clergy in all the churches seemed to have next to no idea as to how to cope with the frankly missionary situation which now faced them', says Welsby.[28]

In 1980 the Alternative Service Book was introduced, as an option alongside the traditional Prayer Book, unrevised since the sixteenth century. The reform was a threat to the Church's uniformity of practice, a basic feature of establishment. Many also saw it as a threat to the Church's social commitment. One critic, the sociologist of religion David Martin, noted that the liturgical reformers

> clearly wish to withdraw from any sense of being embedded in that wider arch of local attachment and loyalty to the 'commonwealth' . . . So the Church becomes merely a pressure group, and loses deep alignments with locality and with nation. This is not to recommend alignments which in the past have

> often been uncritical and unprophetic or to defend
> a traditional Church–State alliance.[29]

The last sentence is disingenuous. The idea of the Church's
organic relation to its surrounding society is pretty obviously due to its history of establishment, which Professor
Martin is therefore implicitly defending.

Robert Runcie was now Archbishop of Canterbury.
He was a very Anglican Archbishop: sceptical, gentle,
humorous and a touch camp. His theology and his politics
were liberal (we will look at his approach to establishment
in Chapter Three). During the early 1980s the Church
acquired a firm image in the public mind: politically left-
wing, doctrinally vague. In other words, the theology of
the 1960s had moved to the centre of Anglicanism, it had
come to define it. The Thatcher government sharpened
the impression: the Church was clearly 'wet'; along
with the BBC and the universities, it was part of 'the
liberal establishment'. It lacked the guts to stand up for
those values that made Britain truly great. The shameful
wetness of this religion was on full display at the Falklands
commemoration service, which carefully shunned tri-
umphalism; and in the *Faith in the City* report of 1985,
clumsily attacked as Marxist.

The government's suspicion did little damage to the
Church's credibility. More serious was the hostility that
came from traditionalist Anglicans. In 1987 a priest called
Garry Bennett committed suicide, having criticised the
Church's leadership in the *Crockford's* Preface. The Church
was submitting to the spirit of the age, he had complained.
There was a period of soul-searching and press analysis.
What did the Church of England now stand for? It now

had an unprecedentedly 'social' emphasis, both domestically and through the worldwide Anglican Communion. This effected a shift in the meaning of the Church's establishment: it was increasingly justified on progressive, mildly socialist grounds. Such a justification was not brand new, but now it had become dominant, decisively ousting the idea of the Church as the Tory Party at prayer. The Church looked more like Her Majesty's Alternative Opposition: aiming to speak for the weaker members of society, and the wider world.

In reality, of course, very many Anglicans were unimpressed by this redefinition of establishment and continued to think of it in the old way. One was Enoch Powell, who made a traditional defence of establishment in the House of Commons in 1984:

> It is possible to have an internally self-governed church in this country, but it will not be the national church, it will not be the Church of England. The Church is the Church of England because of royal supremacy, because there is royal — and that is to say, lay — supremacy. It is for that reason that it is the Church of the people and the Church of the nation, and can never be converted into a mere sect or a private, self-managing corporation.[30]

Most of the bishops would have been slightly uneasy at hearing such a defence. The establishment of the Church had become a deeply contradictory phenomenon.

Arts excursus

Before continuing with the history of Church and state, let us step back, and consider the Church's cultural image, and its role in the arts, in these years.

It seems increasingly clear that the most important post-War English poet is Philip Larkin. Though not a believer, he is a witness to the last generation of cultural Anglicanism. One of his best-known poems, 'Church Going', written in 1955, provides good evidence. Church is no longer habitable; it is an interesting thing to look at rather than a place to look from, a position to occupy. And of course its meaning is humanised, anthropologised; it speaks of deep, serious forces, but one must decode it, demythologise it. Larkin is a post-Anglican poet; his tacit theme is the waning of Anglican culture. His work is sympathetic to many aspects of this culture – the awkward reverence, the social propriety, the vague shame, the half-ironic nationalism, the dislike of enthusiasm and innovation – but without Christian faith. Both 'Church Going' and 'The Whitsun Weddings' speak of the receding religious culture he inhabits. Larkin was clear that, intellectually and emotionally, Christianity simply does not stand up to secular opposition, such as art, jazz, love, sex, being honest. His poetry records, and helps to effect, Anglicanism's removal from mainstream sensibility; its translation into heritage, into paradise lost. (Betjeman was a more enthusiastic Anglican, but the effect of his work was similar.)

The 1970s and 1980s saw the growth of the heritage industry: Laura Ashley, Merchant-Ivory etc. Television often peddled a nostalgic view of England, and the Church of England was more than ever identified with its traditional, rural presence. Its representation by television perpetuated a vaguely 1950s image: the grinning idiot on a bike in *To the Manor Born*, and so on. And of course the TV vicar of the 1990s changed sex but held on to the rural idyll, with the cutsey name of Dibley. At the time of writing, a documentary is being aired, called *A Country Parish*, that reaffirms the rural idyll model of the Church. A nostalgic setting is where the nation wants its Church (or Westminster Abbey).

The Church has not often been represented on *East-Enders* (which is Britain's most popular media experience), except in the context of weddings and funerals. (Incidentally, *Four Weddings and a Funeral* sums up the religious content of British film and TV.) Once or twice religion has featured in *EastEnders* in the form of scary cults seducing teenagers. One might have expected the occasional black character to be a churchgoer, but maybe the writers consider this a counter-aspirational stereotype. Soap-operas are essentially anti-religious, for the simple reason that religious people tend to have less interesting love-lives. Nevertheless one might expect an established Church to have a stronger role in the established soap-opera.

It is hard to think of any British TV programme in which religion is part of the fabric of life, rather than eccentric or sinister. This is in stark contrast to the most popular American import, *The Simpsons*, in which it is considered normal and healthy for the family to attend church. My point is simply that its establishment does not make the Church an established part of popular culture. One could hardly defend establishment on the grounds that it keeps religion before the popular mind. The opposite is surely true: because Christianity is officially privileged, it can be safely marginalised, and mocked. To discriminate against it has the appearance of cultural daring – though in reality it is quintessentially conformist. Radio One, the established pop radio station, automatically bans any songs with religious content, in case the impressionable youths are lured away from their diet of liberally-sanctioned smut. OFCOM, the body that regulates broadcasting, acts as a secular censor, trying to keep all mainstream programming free of religious bias, meaning religion, and to confine religious programmes to a special box.

Serious television is similarly light on intelligent and sympathetic portrayals of the national religion. There is no religious equivalent of Simon Schama or Melvyn Bragg. Television implicitly argues that intelligence is secular; it can only do religion to a sugary formula (*Songs of Praise*).

By about 1980 it was a very rare thing indeed for a literary writer to express Anglican sympathy. Yet it was a cliché to express attachment to the cultural by-products: the old liturgy, the Authorised Version, the choral tradition and sundry other charming Gothic accretions. The novelist and biographer A. N. Wilson reflected on his Anglicanism in an essay of 1986:

> I am glad to belong to the Church of England because it is the Church of *England*. It is the Church to which the majority of my fellow countrymen notionally belong, and to which the great majority of English Christians in the past in fact belonged. I think of all the griefs and wisdom of Samuel Johnson; I think of Jane Austen and Tennyson growing up in their fathers' parsonage houses . . . If I was leaving

the Church of England I would feel I was leaving them.[31]

In other words, the basis of his faith is communion with the literary dead. He soon realised that such communion was available through reading books, and left the Church (in as far as it is possible to leave this Church).

A similar perspective is provided by the playwright Alan Bennett. In his diaries and other writings he criticises the trendification of the Church and camply bemoans its loss of cultural confidence. (This is despite the fact that he helped to dent this confidence in the 1960s with cruel parodies of vicars.) In 1990 he addressed the Prayer Book Society, expressing gentle regret that Cranmer's prose was receding from the cultural memory, that its passing 'has diminished the common stock of shared reference'. He admits that his position is vulnerable, being a semi-lapsed Anglican: the liturgical reformers would argue that it is none of his business. Bennett writes:

> This is the same argument that is advanced by farmers in answer to protests about the grubbing up of hedges and the destruction of field patterns . . . But there is an ecology of belief as well as of nature. Poetry, mystery, the beauty of language – these may be incidental to the primary purpose of the Church, which is to bring people to God, but one doesn't have to be Archbishop Laud to see that these incidental virtues of the Prayer Book are not irrelevant or dispensable.[32]

In other words, the Church should be deeply embedded within the overall culture in order to achieve its spiritual ends. Bennett is guilty of a selective nostalgia for the

religious past: there are surely elements of the loss that he
does not regret. He expresses his analysis of the Church's
predicament in a vivid conceit:

> God [to the liturgical reformers] is like an aged
> father taken in by his well-intentioned children. They
> want to keep him presentable and a useful member
> of society, so they scrap his old three-piece suit, in
> which he looked a little old-fashioned (though rather
> distinguished), and kit him out instead in pastel-
> coloured leisurewear in which he looks like every-
> body else. The trouble is, though, they can't change
> the habits of a lifetime. It's not so much that he spits
> in the fire or takes his teeth out at the table, but
> that, given the chance, he is so forthright. He's
> always laying down the law and seems to think
> nobody else exists, and his family might be servants
> the way he treats them. It's a bit embarrassing –
> particularly when those warm, friendly people from
> the religion next door come round. Still, it's only a
> matter of time. Father's old. He may die soon.[33]

This is worth unpicking for a minute. Bennett's impli-
cation is that the Church is inevitably embarrassingly
archaic: we must suffer its awkward otherness, like good
daughters of King Lear (the obvious unstated allusion).
To seek to modernise it is a sort of hideous impiety. In
fact the Lear analogy is worth developing. Lear becomes
politically weak but refuses to adapt to the fact. Bennett,
like a good romantic, wants us to see this refusal as noble,
but really there is no virtue in failing to adapt to reality.
The fact is that, like Lear, the Church has lost its cultural
authority. Should it nevertheless hang on to its old language of authority? No. It is better off without that old

baggage. Its old voice of authority was impressive but tainted, tainted to the core. Achieving distance from Cranmer was a piece of healthy realism, a liberation. It was a sign of confidence that the Church is *not* essentially a noble relic; that it is not dying but shedding a skin. Bennett's parable is amusing but theologically wrong-headed. And it backfires on him: it is he who resembles Lear's cynical daughters, for effectively he is saying to the Church, 'Being old and weak, seem so!'

Many writers from the Hampstead area enjoy a bit of cultural Anglicanism in middle age. In 1981 Beryl Bainbridge criticised the ASB:

> The Church shouldn't worry about the size of the flock. It should wait, unchanged, on the sidelines . . . A belief in God requires an act of faith, and the sustaining of such an implausible proposition requires that the language and ritual of prayer, of baptism and burial and Communion, should be both mystical and difficult.[34]

The novelist Fay Weldon has recently joined the ranks of the literary dispossessed. After decades on the front line of culture's secularisation, she now warns the Church to keep its distance. 'The more it courts popularity at all costs, the less moral ascendancy it has.' And of course the liturgical reform is blamed: 'The changing prayer-book unsettles people: they like to think of themselves in church as part of an ongoing tradition that has been and will go on. They want to belong to the faith of their fathers (and mothers), and they're not allowed.'[35] Again: the Church should be a force of inspirational cultural authority (as long as we're still allowed to hang on to the secular advances of the last four decades).

But these cultural Anglicans are a mere footnote to the literary scene. The new literary generation of the 1980s included Martin Amis, Julian Barnes, Ian McEwan. There is no substantial depiction of Christian belief in any of the urbane novels these men have produced. (Come to think of it, one of McEwan's novels features a psychotic young fundamentalist.) This refusal to engage with religion is quite an English thing. In contrast, the great American novelists of our age – Bellow, Updike, Roth – are doggedly interested in religion. British writers are embarrassed by it, or in hackneyed revolt: when it comes to religion, they are stuck in adolescence.

Recently, Martin Amis recounted an experience familiar to millions of his generation:

> I was six or seven years old, and I was filling out a school registration form, and I came to the disquieting question. I ran into the hall and shouted up the stairs, 'Mum! What religion am I?' There was a long silence, then: 'Uh . . . Church of England!' Yes, thank God for the Church of England: it didn't commit you to anything at all.[36]

It is curious that Amis never became more interested in religion (aren't writers meant to be interested in what makes other people tick?). Instead he epitomises the liberal stance of being aggressively uninterested in religion; annoyed that it exists, muddying the waters of politics and art. In the same article he explains that he became an atheist at the age of twelve, dismissing religion as 'an affront to common sense . . . it seemed an open-and-shut case.' Though he now calls himself an agnostic, his position has hardly changed since his boyhood revelation. 'Belief is otiose; reality is sufficiently awesome as it stands'; every religion 'is a massive agglutination of stock response, of clichés, of inherited and unexamined formulations'. The antidote, of course, is art.

Many writers have remained loyal to religion as a provider of Gothic horror. The novel by Jeanette Winterson, *Oranges are not the Only Fruit*, is a well-known example. The stifling religious upbringing has also featured in many memoirs – and in most cases the power of a literary education is the redeeming force. The basic narrative is How Literature Saved Me From The Darkness of Religion. Literature, and the arts in general, have become more firmly established than ever as the secular faith of the middle classes. The secularisation of literature is reflected in the office of poet laureate. After Betjeman he was no longer expected to have Anglican sympathies in any substantial sense. Ted Hughes was cheerfully neopagan (though he doubtless came out for Cranmer). Andrew Motion is painfully liberal.

What about R. S. Thomas and now Rowan Williams, two well-known Anglican poets from Wales? I hope it does not seem Celtophobic to suggest that their achievements are marginal to my theme: the demise of Anglicanism from the national culture. Others might want to cite Geoffrey Hill, but his tortuous inaccessibility surely helps to prove the cultural marginalisation of the 'established' religion. Who speaks for Anglicanism with any clarity or confidence? In journalism, there are many secularist columnists and many Roman Catholic ones; I can't think of any Anglican ones except for the wholesome opponent of homosexuality Anne Atkins.

The running theme in these reflections is that our nation's cultural life, high and low, almost entirely ignores the fact that we have an established religion: the main response is embarrassment. A final indication: an anthology of Anglican writings was reviewed in the *TLS* in December 2001. There is no doubt, said the reviewer, 'that the Anglican tradition is a living and vibrant one: the best writers of the past forty years – Alan Ecclestone, Austin Farrer, Michael Ramsey, R. S. Thomas, John V. Taylor, W. H. Vanstone – give us much to be grateful for.'[37] It is unlikely that a well-read humanities graduate would have heard of any of these, beside possibly Thomas.

It is crucial that we see afresh the sheer absurdity and embarrassment entailed in the fact that our officially established religion is almost beneath the contempt of our actual culture. Let us be honest: our established religion is the BBC.

The Carey Years

In 1991 George Carey was appointed to Canterbury. It is thought that Mrs Thatcher blocked the Church's favoured candidate, John Habgood. Carey was an Evangelical; he had transformed his Durham parish enthusiastically during the 1980s. This was the sort of appointment that Fisher, Ramsey and Runcie had prayed never to see. It was a shock to the liberals who had grown comfortable under Runcie: they did not like to be reminded that such Anglicans existed. In reality, for many years, the Evangelicals had been on the rise.

Carey was not a natural establishment figure. He came from a 'humble' background and did not go to Oxbridge – much of the savage criticism he endured from the press contained a hint of snobbery. As an Evangelical, Carey was less imbued with the establishment ethos than most of his predecessors. Before he moved to Canterbury, he sounded ambiguous about the idea of a Christian society:

> We are no longer living in a society which we all may safely assume to be a Christian land. We are living in a secular society with fragile links with the Christian faith which once nourished its laws, customs and morals. Our context, therefore, is most emphatically missionary and the role of ministry has shifted from pastoral ministrations to outreach and mission.[38]

This is the classic Evangelical line: mission is the *raison d'être* of the Church. But of course Anglican Evangelicals assume that establishment helps mission. Carey conforms to type, affirming that 'we are very fortunate to have the voice as the established Church'. And he uses the inclusive argument: 'the Church of England does not only minister to its members but to all people in its society. Our Church is here not primarily to make pew fodder but to be salt and light in society and to lead people to faith.'[39] He wants it both ways: the Church is a radical movement, distinct from society at large. Yet it also, rightfully, speaks for society at large.

The defence of 'naturally Anglican Britain' was becoming an embarrassing task. A particularly problematic statistic emerged in 1992: there were just under 2 million Anglicans, and just over 2 million Roman Catholics. Peter Clarke comments, 'It is hardly too much to say that during the twentieth century Great Britain lost its historic identity as a Protestant nation.'[40]

There can be little doubt that the accession of Carey was a huge turning-point for the Church. For he symbolised a trend that had been building up for years: the demise of the centre-ground. During the Runcie years, it was known that there was internal divergence, but it also seemed that there was enough middle ground to contain it. The narrative of the Anglican settlement, the middle way, remained convincing. There was still a dominant Anglican *style*, which Runcie himself embodied very effectively. But now the Church's old image, as a familiar, unthreatening presence, was going. Most obviously, the notion of 'mainstream Anglican worship' seemed to be under threat. Peter Hitchens writes:

> By the early 1990s a worshipper moving from church to church even in the same city, would not have hoped or even expected to find anything more than a vague similarity in the services he encountered. Bibles, prayers, hymns, styles of music, arrangement of the building . . . would all have been entirely unpredictable . . . He might see people speaking "in tongues" or rolling upon the floor, or confessing in public to having partaken of oral sex. He might hear traditional Victorian hymns or a guitar. He might be choked by incense or urged to get up and down five times a minute and shout.[41]

Similar diversity might have existed during the 1980s, but now it seemed to have reached a new level. The Alternative Service Book was one factor, as we have seen, but a much bigger one was the rise of the Evangelicals. Their style was distinctly un-Anglican, combining a high level of commitment with almost total informality.

Something should be said about Anglican Evangelical ecclesiology. It is notoriously problematic. Part of the rhetorical repertoire of a British Evangelical preacher is to distinguish Christianity from 'going to church on

Sunday'. The Evangelicals need 'church' to kick against, to provide a foil for the *surprising* relevance and realism of the Gospel. Of course, they then proceed to give a new account of church, as the community of the faithful. And if they are Anglicans, they will admit the importance of the worldwide catholic and apostolic Church, and explain how the dear old institution might be redeemable after all.

Anglican Evangelicals have always had a difficult relationship with their Church. They have felt, rightly, looked down on by the Anglo-Catholics and liberals. Look at Trollope's amazing snobbery; his depiction of absolute monsters in dog-collars. When they have tried to get involved in the institution they have been accused of trying to take it over; when they have retreated they have been called sectarian. In the 1950s they once again emerged from the woodwork, brandishing a large persecution complex. Their leading theologian, John Stott, spoke of the Church of England as 'the best boat to fish from'. This seemed proof that Evangelicals saw the church as the means to an end – saving souls – and had no respect for its traditional and sacramental life. Gradually this changed: the Keele Congress of Anglican Evangelicals in 1967 was a big step towards a more positive acceptance of Anglican ecclesiology.

But the energy of the modern Evangelical movement remains essentially congregational. Authority lies in the immediate congregation of worshippers as it is led by the Spirit. There are obvious dangers here of sectarianism, puritanism and charismatic leadership. There is a constant quest for a pure church, defined by the observance of strict rules gleaned from the Bible, and close fellowship. Anglicanism has always tried to repress this tendency; to emphasise that authority is 'dispersed', in bishops, in the crown, and in the universal catholic Church (traditionally, of course, it imagines authority coming downwards from bishops to priests to congregations). It has also pointed to tradition and reason as authorities alongside Scripture. Anglican Evangelicals take little notice of this; they begin with the individual's relationship with God, then talk about the congregation, and finally, rather vaguely, about the Church in general.

Good evidence of this is provided by the most influential Anglican of recent years, Nicky Gumbel, who made the Alpha movement such a success in the 1990s. His book *Questions of Life* is aimed at the absolute beginner, so it should not be read as definitive of his theology, but it is nevertheless a useful guide to his approach. After thirteen short chapters about the individual's relationship with God there is a chapter called 'What About the Church?' The old, irrelevant model of church is now confronted: 'Hard pews, unsingable tunes, enforced silence and excruciating boredom are just a few ingredients that make up the common image of church on Sunday.'[42] This fusty old model is now being challenged by a new sort of church, he reports: 'Many churches are now creating a wonderfully warm and outward-going Christian family which is much closer to the biblical picture.'[43] In other words, church is the getting-together of dynamic, committed Christians. The high ecclesiology of Anglicanism is implicitly rejected, a form of congregationalism is embraced.

Another development in these years was financial. The Church lost a billion pounds in the early 1990s. This put more pressure on congregations to raise their 'quota', paid to central organisation. Appeals for regular giving became more insistent, and added to the sense of the congregation as a highly committed club. As congregations became smaller, an increasing amount was expected, in terms of time, money and attitude, from those who remained. Robert Van de Weyer says, 'A few people – a diminishing few – are willing to pay this fee; and some gain great satisfaction in doing so. But as the fee has gone up and up, so more and more people are staying out of the club.'[44] This, according to one analyst, largely accounts for the decline in attendance figures. 'As the clergy have become doctrinally stricter, the liberals, instead of staying to register dissent, have preferred to vote with their feet and a new generation of liberals sympathetic to Christianity has not joined.'[45] In a vicious circle, dwindling congregations became more committed, and fringe-members have felt less welcome.

In the 1990s the Church not only turned inward for a stronger sense of identity, it also turned abroad. Runcie had celebrated the diversity of the Anglican Communion. Carey was more interested in harnessing the strength of distant churches, and even importing aspects of their theology. 'In the UK, organised Christianity has been declining since the war by 60,000 members a year', Carey admitted. 'Yet the worldwide picture is very different – there the Church is growing by 80,000 Christians a day! Those churches that are growing would put us to shame by their life, their richness and their bold, uncompromising faith.'[46] Yes, and their distinctly pre-liberal approach to many moral issues.

In November 1992 General Synod voted for the ordination of women. The vote was a kick in the groin for traditionalists. Many Tory MPs and journalists discovered that their previous doubts about papal authority were

misguided. One defector was the former Bishop of
London, Graham Leonard (who, incidentally, confirmed
me – does that put my confirmation in doubt?). 'The
Church of England cannot claim to be anything more than
a sect,' he now said. 'It may be the Established Sect: but
theologically it is now a sect.'[47]

The crisis raised fresh questions about establishment.
William Rees-Mogg, a Catholic journalist, warned of a
'national institutional crisis. In part it involves the
unwinding of the original compromise which combined
Catholic and Protestant elements in a single state
church'.[48] Forward in Faith was formed; it demanded that
opposition to women priests should be tolerated. The
demand was met, which meant that a serious schism
(sorry, 'impairment of communion') in the Church was
accepted. Carey called the dissenters heretics, and had to
withdraw the comment. The incident revealed that the
Church had become essentially unleadable: the attempt
to impose uniformity on it was merely counter-
productive.

In 1977 the theologian Stephen Sykes had written a
defence of the middle way called *The Integrity of Anglicanism*, a title now in danger of sounding ironic. In 1992,
now Bishop of Ely, he admitted that the situation looked
increasingly grave:

> It is not unreasonable to ask whether the situation
> today is not worse than before, whether the slow
> erosion of Christian belief and practice in England
> is not closely connected to the incoherence of a
> Church which disputes publicly about its essential or
> fundamental doctrines, and whether the removal of
> the cement provided by establishment would not

precipitate the end of the Anglican experiment altogether.[49]

As well as suffering the exodus over women priests, Carey was also under assault from his own side. In 1993 the Evangelical lobby Reform was founded. The year before, various Evangelical churches had imposed caps on the quotas they paid to the central organisation. Their major complaint was homosexuality. To Evangelicals, women priests are just about tolerable; gay ones are not. Paul's anti-feminism is less precious to them than his homophobia. The Evangelicals were angry that, even with an Evangelical Archbishop in Canterbury, the Church was not returning to 'traditional Christian morality', but continuing its gradual liberalisation. The protest was in vain. The fact is that Anglican conservatives were fatally wrong-footed by the liberal legislation of the sixties. In a permissive society, the established Church is necessarily a permissive Church: otherwise it advocates social policies at odds with the law of the land and becomes a reactionary sect. This is why many liberals fear disestablishment, despite knowing in their hearts it is right: it would jeopardise the Church's commitment to the liberal values of the cultural mainstream. The fear is understandable, but it is no excuse to cling on to establishment. Fear should not determine our conception of the Church.

The D-Word

Let us sum up the situation of the early 1990s. The Church's internal division was more serious than at any time since the 1850s. Again, the Church seemed to need a strong centrist movement which could reunite it through a renewed emphasis on its national role. Or, to put the matter differently, the very last thing it needed right now was a long-running scandal casting doubt on its constitutional feasibility. Enter the new Anne Boleyn.

Until 1993, disestablishment was, to the secular press, just a humorously long and archaic word; something their grandfathers used to get worked up about. What put it in the headlines was not anything going on within the Church itself, but something infinitely more interesting to the public: the separation of the Prince and Princess of Wales in 1992.

Charles and Diana's wedding was, according to Runcie, 'the stuff of fairy-tales'. (Beauty and the Beast?) When they take their vows, he had said in 1981, 'they will be doing so as representative figures for the nation'.[50] (In private Runcie was a bit worried about this unlikely match.) Let us pass over the history of the world's un-happiest marriage. This national 'sacrament' ended in public adultery and tabloid sleaze. More to the point, it ended in a constitutional conundrum. It looked like the heir to the throne would soon be seeking to remarry – and to remarry someone who was herself divorced. The Church was opposed to the remarriage of divorcees.

In 1936, marriage to a divorced person was deemed to be impossible for a member of the royal family; a judgement confirmed in 1955. Now, however, it looked like Charles was intending to overturn this verdict. What was the Church to say? It could not agree to remarry Charles; but on the other hand it did not dare denounce his relationship with Camilla Parker-Bowles, which quickly became public knowledge. This speaks volumes about the loss of the Church's cultural authority. In the cases of Edward VIII and Princess Margaret, the enamoured royal had to give way to the rock-like Church. Now the assumption was that the Church would have to adapt itself to the lively love-life of royalty. Which it has duly done: its position on remarriage has conveniently softened over the last few years.

In January 1993 the *Economist* declared that, for the first time in years, 'politicians and newspapers of all stripes are discussing whether disestablishment of the Church of England might benefit monarchy, church and nation'. A debate about the wider issue duly began. The radical priest Ken Leech spoke for many on the Anglican Left. He confronted the claim that a disestablished Church would be reduced to a mere sect and would lose its universal reach:

> As someone who has lived and/or worked in inner city areas for the whole of my life, I find this a strange claim. If the Anglican presence is only sustained by a legal structure, is it worth anything? Experience in the US suggests that presence in and commitment to an area has more to do with fundamental belief, with theology, than it has with legal apparatus . . . Were it to be disestablished, the Church of England might well lose some of its more expensive buildings and much of its status, but what it might gain in credibility is enormous . . . As it stands the Church of England is a compromised, captivated and Constantinian church, a church in bondage to Babylon, a church which is bound to have safe leaders: its bishops are state nominees. Charming and pleasant as they are, they bear the mark of the beast . . . For the Church to hide behind the structures of Caesar is a betrayal of the Gospel.[51]

The Archbishop of York wore his mark of the beast with pride. He wrote a letter to the *Times* laying out the major arguments against disestablishment:

> First, such a development would rightly be seen as signifying that the nation was formally repudiating the Christian heritage and was no longer prepared to pay even lip service to those Christian beliefs and values on which so much of its history and the best of its life have been based. Secondly, beyond the ranks of regular week-by-week Anglican church-goers, there are millions who regard the Church of England as 'our' church and who seek its ministry, not only for their weddings or funerals or baptism, but often at times of stress or trouble or thanksgiving in their lives. Thirdly, for the most part members of other Christian churches, and indeed of other faiths now present in this country, are not in favour of disestablishment. On the contrary, to a degree which is not widely enough understood, their leaders often see the fact of establishment as enabling the Church of England to be in the vanguard of action with them or on their behalf on matters of common concern.[52]

The strongest call for disestablishment from a senior Anglican figure came in 1994. Colin Buchanan, Bishop of Woolwich, wrote a book called *Cut the Connection*, which set the case out clearly. We have reached the final phase in the story of establishment, he announced, in which its defenders are committed to wilful pretence:

> There is the pretence that we are in 'partnership' with the State, when we are in fact in captivity;

there is the pretence that, if in any one or two years we have not encountered that State control in its most virulent form, it has actually gone away; and there is the ostrich-like insistence that all reforms that have happened up until the present moment have been enlightened and welcome, but all proposed for the future are destructive of the fabric of the Church or of society or of both. Are we really arrived at the most enlightened form, the most delicate balance, of relationships between Church and State that all changes proposed for the future must be harmful? Or can we actually call an end to pretence and a dawning of reality?[53]

Buchanan attacks the arguments of Habgood that we just noted; in particular the idea that establishment is justified by its contribution to social cohesion and national identity. 'We appear to be approaching a wholly pragmatic basis for establishment, an establishment in which the Church accepts State control *for the sake of the State.*'[54] And it is not the Church's calling to be a symbol of the nation:

a kind of mascot-cum-coat-of-arms role for the Church of England . . . has no warrant in the New Testament, appears to lose sight of Jesus Christ himself, and in passing dispenses with any argument from numbers – we can be but a tiny minority, it seems to be saying, but if that tiny minority (perhaps, say, like Yeomen of the Guard?) can encapsulate from history some role of 'carrying national identity', then . . . there never ever could be a reason to disestablish.[55]

Over the next few years the possibility of constitutional

change seemed to be increasing, and the prime advocate seemed to be the Prince of Wales himself. Charles wanted to downplay his future role as head of the Church; he spoke about the title 'Defender of the Faith' in his 1994 television interview: 'I personally would rather see it as Defender of Faith, not the Faith . . . People have fought each other to the death over these things, which seems to me a peculiar waste of people's energy, when we're all actually aiming for the same ultimate goal, I think.' He thus wanted the title to mean the direct opposite of what it formerly did: not the figurehead and champion of a particular religion, but the champion of religious tolerance. There was much talk about how his coronation oath would have to be changed: should it be enlarged to include all forms of Christianity? That would mean the repeal of the Act of Succession, which banned Catholics from the throne. In 1995 Charles had explicitly questioned this: 'I really can't think why we can't have Catholics on the throne.'[56] In 1997 he was beginning to attend public social engagements with Camilla. The issue was still unresolved: Dr Carey said that the prospect of a marriage was likely to 'create a crisis for the Church'.

In August 1997 Diana died. The Di-dolatry that ensued was widely seen as the nation's biggest surge of religious feeling for decades. The Roman Catholic journalist Paul Johnson had a pop at the Church of England: 'The effect of Diana's short life did more to promote Christian values in this country than all the efforts of our state church in half a century.'[57] The funeral, at which Diana's brother tried to deify the deceased, Elton John sang, and people clapped, symbolised the sad lot of the national Church. To stay at the heart of national life, it had to pander to popular sentiment, rather like the royal family doing *It's a Knockout.* A couple of years later it suffered a similar humiliation, when the two-thousandth anniversary of Christ's birth was celebrated at the Millennium Dome. The Queen was invited to sing an alternative, modern anthem, 'All you need is love' – a dictum which is in direct contradiction to the Christian message.

The millennium celebrations raised acute questions about British, and English, identity. The Blair government had devolved power to Scotland and Wales, and British sovereignty continued to leak away to Europe. The problem of British, and English, identity was intensified by the crisis threatening Crown and Church. In January 1999 the *Independent on Sunday* reported that a new ecumenical coronation service was being devised, letting Charles off the Protestant hook. Its leading article pronounced disestablishment to be 'an historical inevitability', and found supporting evidence in regional devolution: 'If the Kingdom is to be disunited, as it clearly is, then the Church can hardly avoid disestablishment . . . [T]he Prime Minister should make coherent plans for a post-Anglican, post-Christian settlement.'[58]

At the end of the Decade of Evangelism, things looked worse than ever for the Church. For the first time, Sunday attendance fell below the one million mark. And the decline in folk religion was even more striking. In 1960 over half of all English babies were baptised, by 2000 around a tenth. Over this time the proportion of marriages taking place in the Church of England halved. In 1957, 55 per cent of the population had said that they belonged to the Church of England; in 2000 the figure was 25 per cent. For most, the Church had ceased to be part of daily life.

While the problem of Charles' marital status lurked in

the background, another challenge to establishment arose. One aspect of establishment is the Church's representation in the House of Lords – it has 26 bishops there. In its 1997 manifesto Labour had promised to replace the House of Lords with an elected chamber. In 2000 it asked the Wakeham Commission to propose a solution, and the Church to state its case. At July's General Synod, Michael Turnbull, the Bishop of Durham, made a sturdy defence of the *status quo*, which was presented not as a piece of privilege but as a service to the nation. Synod followed his lead and advised Wakeham not to cut its bishops. But the commission proposed to reduce the number of bishops to 16, to introduce 5 of other denominations and 5 of other faiths. In the end its proposal was rejected by the House of Commons and reform was stalled. What emerges from the episode is the Church's determination to defend its position, and to present this as altruistic. Incidentally, defenders of establishment often assert that other faith communities are in favour of it. The Wakeham Commission canvassed the views of 30 faith communities on the question of religious representation in the Lords, and all who responded were opposed to the *status quo* – all except the Church of England and the Scottish Episcopal Church.

There is no need to relate what happened in September 2001. It jolted many people into thinking afresh about the relationship between religion and culture, the present author included. The media's reaction to the terrorist outrage was predictably awkward. There was obviously a strong will to condemn religious fanaticism, yet there was an equally strong fear of sounding Islamophobic. Outspoken secularists such as Polly Toynbee and Richard Dawkins launched angry attacks against religion in general.

They were further irked by the government's response to the crisis. The Home Secretary David Blunkett suggested that the blasphemy law should be widened to protect all religious groups, in an attempt to guard against an anti-Islamic reaction. Free speech seemed under threat from religious sensitivity.

Another hot issue was faith schools. In June the Church had published the Dearing Report which affirmed that 'Church schools stand at the centre of the Church's mission to the nation.' Subsequently the government announced the creation of more faith schools, to increase the proportion from roughly one in five. This was especially controversial because educational separatism had been widely blamed for contributing to the previous summer's northern riots. Why, some people asked, was the government helping to establish separate faith ghettoes? Surely this would only prevent the integration of minorities, foster fanaticism and cause resentment in the wider culture?

The government's religious policy was therefore to encourage religious separatism, to weaken the idea of a common culture that applies across the religious board. Many saw this as the exact opposite of what was needed. Surely the US had a healthier model of national identity, due to their official exclusion of religion from the constitution? Thanks to Britain's religious establishment, there was no way of affirming national identity without offending multicultural sensitivity. The columnist Libby Purves identified the problem, or part of it:

> Lukewarm yet official faith impedes us: we feel an awkward chivalry because Christianity is dominant. For, weak as it is, religion in Britain clings creepily

to the appearance of secular power through anach-
ronisms like the established Church and the PM's
voice in selecting an archbishop. This makes it infinitely harder for UK governments to swat aside
barbarities which emerge from other faiths, saying
'Religion is between you and God, but it is never
above the law of the land'.[59]

After Carey

During 2002 disestablishment became a hotter media topic
than ever. The reason was the resignation of Dr Carey
and the protracted public choosing of his replacement.
This reminded the media of the prime minister's role in
the appointment: some newspapers and commentators
declared for disestablishment. 'More and more people
outside the Church of England seem to find it preposterous that the British Prime Minister is about to
play a crucial role in selecting the next Archbishop of
Canterbury', noted Clifford Longley. 'They do not wish
to be involved in the internal processes of one particular
religious organization: the proposition is offensive to
them, and in principle also offensive to Anglicans. The
fact that not enough of the latter are offended is deeply
worrying.' He noted that the 'creeping disestablishment'
of the 1970s had stopped in recent years: 'it appears that
the leaders of the Church of England have decided to dig
in on the present line – thus far and no further'.[60]

In the *Guardian* Hywel Williams put the case. 'A
century and a half after Cavour talked about the need for
"a free church in a free state", Anglican establishment
remains preposterous and harmful to the church itself. In
Oxford and Cambridge, the Anglican-linked jobs for the

boys and girls have seen Anglican scholarship dwindle. As for spiritual leadership, Cardinal Hume was a reproach to the comparative Anglican hollowness.' He listed various pieces of archaic state pageantry: 'These antics remain the public face of England's church, however great the practical priest's identification with the poor and the outcast.'[61]

Other voices for change included the columnists Libby Purves and Simon Jenkins, both of *The Times*. At the risk of sounding ungracious, it might be observed that some of these calls for disestablishment are rather facile. Do such commentators understand the scale of the theological revolution entailed? Do they understand that all Christianity naturally gravitates towards expecting to be established in some way or other, as its birthright? For example, Longley and Purves are Catholics. When has Catholicism ever willingly turned down political privilege? English Catholics are like teenage aristocrats slumming it. They have the benefits of nonconformist status, but the deep-rooted sense that their religion is meant to be culturally empowered. And for secularists to oppose establishment is about as daring as opposing world hunger. Slightly more daringly, Mark Santer, the retiring Bishop of Birmingham, declared for disestablishment – the first diocesan bishop to do so since Hensley Henson in the 1920s.

During these months, Carey repeatedly restated his belief in establishment. The intention was to block Williams, widely perceived as the most liberal candidate on this issue (we will look into this in Chapter Three). A mutual antipathy between Carey and Williams was common knowledge. Four years earlier Carey had blocked Williams' appointment to Southwark, on account of his liberalism on homosexuality. 'Removing the spiritual underpinning of the State', he said in April, 'would inevitably tend to cast religion as a purely private matter, one of a range of lifestyle options, like buying organic food or living in the country, of no greater public or communal import than, say, stamp collecting or birdwatching.'[62] Does this mean that other religions and denominations are trivial? Or are they saved from triviality by the Church of England's establishment? Either way, it seems rather ill-considered. 'From the perspective of the Church of England', Dr Carey continued, 'establishment helps to underwrite the commitment of a national Church to serve the entire community.'

A similar case was made by Michael Turnbull, Bishop of Durham (who has since retired). He explained that parliamentary influence over the Church is not to be regretted: it 'has proved a useful corrective for a church which can become blinkered to its wider obligations.'[63] And he proceeds to remind the Church of these obligations. 'Among all the Christian denominations and the growing significance of wider faith communities, the Church of England has a unique vocation of its own. It is to serve the nation from within the major institutions which are the framework of our society.' Any student of twentieth-century history will be uneasy about this rhetoric. For the 'German Christians' in the 1930s claimed a 'special vocation' to combine the Gospel with patriotic feeling. There is no divine warrant for politicising the Gospel.

In June it was leaked that Williams was the first choice of the Crown Appointments Commission. The indiscretion made the whole process seem even more absurd. In July Williams' appointment was confirmed.

At July's Synod, the issue of the appointment of bishops

happened to be on the agenda, scheduled the previous year. Colin Buchanan, the Bishop of Woolwich, a long-standing campaigner for disestablishment, whose book we have already cited, proposed that the monarch and the prime minister be entirely removed from the appointments procedure – a large step towards disestablishment. Of course the motion stood no chance, especially now. Paradoxically, the issue was too topical to receive proper treatment. The Bishop of Worcester, Peter Selby, was one of the few who bothered stating the case for change, calling the present system 'wrong in principle, politically dangerous, ecumenically embarrassing, and theologically indefensible'. But the day was won by people like the Very Reverend Colin Slee, who said the following: 'This is the Golden Jubilee of Her Majesty the Queen. By rejecting this motion, synod has a golden opportunity of showing its loyalty. The motion is a Trojan horse towards the disestablishment of the Church, whatever blandishments we might hear.'[1] Buchanan restated his case in the press:

> It is screamingly inappropriate for the political leader who emerges by vote from the governing party in the House of Commons to have thereby the power to make or to block the candidates for leadership in the Church of England . . . The manoeuvrings in the current archiepiscopal vacancy have highlighted the sorry state of our episcopal appointments procedures, and the crying need for their reform. Oh that we could be free to decide for ourselves our spiritual leaders before God![65]

In February 2003, Rowan Williams was enthroned. It was an upbeat event, with Welsh harping and African drumming. The press sounded more positive about the Church than it had for decades. A leading article in the *Guardian* the next day began with the recent census finding that a significant majority (71.7 per cent) of Britons called themselves Christians:

> This is a Christian country . . . Just as the census reveals a huge network of professed Christians across the country, so the Church of England still maintains, often against the odds, one of the largest institutional networks in the country. Post Offices and local shops may relocate elsewhere, but the church stays put, in the village and the inner city alike, doing the job and acting to bind the social fabric, at the heart of everything from education to music making.

And it asked its readers to consider the possibility that 'the church has a more vital role to play in the search for community and personal peace than has sometimes been allowed recently.' A year earlier, when the selection of a new primate was beginning, a *Guardian* leader had called for disestablishment in no uncertain terms, and various of its columnists joined the call. This reflects the difficulty in being consistent and clear-eyed about this institution. The Church's critics fall into a sort of schizophrenia. One day they will indignantly demand disestablishment, but not long after they will perpetuate the rhetoric of the Church as national-social-unifier.

What is the significance of this 72 per cent vote of confidence in Christianity? To many, it proves that Britain remains a Christian nation and that establishment is there- fore justified. There are various problems with this. Firstly, the allegiance to Christianity seems very largely cultural rather than religious. The Soul Of Britain survey, com-

missioned by the BBC in 2001, found that only 27 per
cent believed in a personal God of any sort. Secondly, it
is not, of course, a majority vote for the Anglican Church,
which has slightly less allegiance than the Roman Catholic
Church in terms of actual attendance. Thirdly, one
wonders at what point such a statistic would prove establishment unjustified. If nominal identification with
Christianity slipped to 50 per cent, would an established
Church still make sense? The point is that, until recently,
the nation's identification with Christianity was assumed
to be very close to 100 per cent. The numbers game is
a dangerous one for establishment-advocates to play.

The week after Williams' enthronement, Richard
Harries, Bishop of Oxford, gave a lecture on 'Church and
State' at St Bride's, Fleet Street. He gave an account of
the recent history of establishment and predicted that
there were more changes to come. But these changes
need not mean disestablishment. Of course, disestablishment might happen (if the monarchy were abolished or
lost its ecclesiastical role). If it did, the Church would be
fine, it would flourish, he said, with a confident wave of
the hand. But what a shame for the state! He referred to
all the Catholics and Hindus who were huge fans of
establishment. He pointed out how useful it was in the
organisation of local civic ceremonies. He pointed out
that Parliament opened with a prayer every day – a
recognition that there was something beyond politics. He
also admitted that establishment had advantages for the
Church. In particular, it gave the Church a bigger voice
in society. When bishops speak, the media tends to listen.
'In America, on the other hand, where religion is so big,
the bishops are not given the same sort of attention.'

(This implies that it is more important for bishops to have high status than it is for religion to be popular.)

The idea that the Church must advocate establishment not for its own sake but for the sake of others strikes me as deeply objectionable. I hope I wasn't *too* rude. At question time I got in first. Might it not be that a true Christian church was autonomous, that it existed to serve God rather than any political order? He calmly informed me that the alternative to an established church is one focused on a papacy. Not in the case of Protestant churches, I said. Well, the other extreme is sects. That seemed to settle it. He said that establishment had nothing to do with 'crude nationalism'. With subtle nationalism, then? I asked, rudely. Someone else asked him if he thought the idea of Christendom was still valid. No, of course not, he replied, like a brave modernist; it died centuries ago. But what else is an established Church but a mouldy piece of Christendom? (I didn't ask that out loud.)

In March Britain sided with the US rather than the UN and invaded Iraq. The new Archbishop of Canterbury, along with other church leaders, had warned that such a war would be unjust. The previous July he had signed a petition calling a potential invasion without UN backing immoral and illegal. Once the war started, various bishops made a point of saying that prayers for victory would be inappropriate. This says much about the awkward position of the established Church. It has a voice that is widely heard but safely ignored. Also, its principled stand against this war sits uneasily with its supply of army chaplains to the troops. There is no escaping the fact that some sort of blessing is conferred by the presence of such chaplains.

After his strong anti-war stance, Williams tried to seem even-handed. He told the chaplains that they stood 'in a long and honourable tradition of Christians bearing witness to the love of Christ in hard and dangerous places.' As Williams himself was doubtless painfully aware, this won't really do.

As we have seen throughout this chapter, an established Church in an effectively secular state is in an odd position. Not only does it have to tolerate what is objectionable to it; it implicitly gives its blessing to every other limb of state: to government policy, to the output of the BBC, to the National Lottery (which a few bishops wetly protested about at first), and so on. In return, of course, it is allowed to cling on to some of its old cultural influence. This difficult, perhaps compromised, position is the Church's duty, say the defenders of establishment (they might reach for an 'incarnational' theology at this point). I am daring to accuse this argument of being sub-Christian. It presupposes that principle must be compromised for the attainment of cultural power. Politicians rightly make this sort of calculation, Christians wrongly. When principle and power are in conflict, Christianity chooses principle every time. It would rather be weak than compromised. It would rather die than translate the Gospel of Jesus Christ into political pragmatism. Humanly speaking this is naïve, it even seems suicidal, but the Church trusts in God to sustain it.

This is really the basic argument for disestablishment: an established Church gives its blessing, which is Christ's blessing, to the dirty little productions of the state. It therefore becomes hampered in its one and only task: to communicate the authority of God in Jesus Christ. It is a question of authority. The Gospel must be purged of its associations with worldly authority. This is doubtless an ongoing task that will never be fully complete in this world. But that is no excuse for delay.

Any church which does delay is the Grand Inquisitor of Dostoyevsky's famous parable, who knowingly combines the Gospel with worldly authority. How often have I heard this tale cited and glossed by well-endowed churchmen! Over the last few decades there has been endless Anglican talk about the need for a prophetic Church that sides with the weak, that is free of the Constantinian compromise, and so on. One is tired of it.

Chapter Two

HOOKER'S GHOST:
THE ANGLICAN CENTURIES

HERE FOLLOWS A PARTIAL retelling of four hundred years of Anglican history. As hinted in my introduction, the question of establishment is related to the ever-lively struggle between Protestant and Catholic.

In the sixteenth century, England replaced one form of religious establishment with another. In the process she became a self-contained, recognisably modern state. What was the nature of the old form of religious establishment? A brief answer is provided by one of its last defenders, Thomas More. His Christian name refers us back to another symbol of the old order: Thomas Becket. Both Thomases died defending the principle that secular power was subject to the spiritual authority of the Roman Church. If the king tried to usurp this power he committed the fundamental heresy – denial of the authority of the Church. The unity of Christendom depended on each ruler seeing himself as a creature of the Church rather than his own man. This was the old understanding of establishment, shared by Thomas Becket and Thomas More.

But for More there was an added motive for safeguarding the *status quo*. The unity of Christendom was beginning to yield unprecedented cultural fruits: a new era of enlightenment. His hatred of the Lutheran revolt was, in part, the scholar's hatred of the book-burning barbarian. Like his fellow humanists Erasmus and Colet, he was well aware that the Church needed reforming, that it contained pockets of terrible corruption. He grew up during the papacy of Alexander VI, a famous villain, and closer to home, cynical career-priests were tarnishing the name of the Church.

In 1529 More wrote *A Dialogue Concerning Heresies*, an attack on the new theology that was seeping in from Germany. Citing the recent Peasants' War on the Continent, he accused Lutheranism of being naturally chaos-prone, of spawning violence. (This is very like Burke's reaction to the French Revolution.) This justified Lutheranism's violent suppression – which was among More's duties as Henry's Lord Chancellor.

At this time, condemning Lutheranism was still government policy. Nine years earlier Henry himself had put his name to a tract condemning Luther, and the pope had awarded him the title 'Defender of the Faith' for his efforts. Since then he had lived up to the title by proscribing Tyndale's New Testament. Though England remained officially anti-Reformation in 1529, the wind was changing. Henry had decided on divorcing Catherine and marrying Anne, and was seeking a legal means. He was growing impatient: Wolsey was dismissed for his failure to get things moving, and Parliament was called. In 1530 Henry began his assault on Church power; he demanded the appointment to Canterbury of Cranmer, an evangelical sympathiser: the pope unwisely agreed. By 1533 Anne was pregnant, and the royal grip on the Church tightened.

The Act in Restraint of Appeals made Henry head of the Church – or rather, it discovered that he naturally was. For 'by divers sundry old authentic histories and chronicles it is manifestly declared and expressed that this realm of England is an empire . . . governed by one supreme head and king'.[1] Papal interference was presented as a recent anomaly, a newfangled error (like the power of Brussels today). The English Church had always been 'sufficient and meet of itself, without the intermeddling of any exterior person or persons, to declare and determine all such doubts, and to administer all such offices and duties, as to their rooms spiritual doth appertain; for the due administration whereof, and to keep them from corruption and sinister affection, the [monarchy and nobility] have sufficiently endowed the said Church, both with honour and possessions . . .' Here is the first justification of the new-style national Church. The Church is part of the 'body politic', it is asserted. The English Reformation is partly influenced by Renaissance humanism, with its classical republican ideal: Machiavelli lurks in the background as well as Luther.

Following this Act, Anne's coronation went ahead, in direct defiance of the pope. More looked on with horror: since he had written against Lutheranism four years earlier, a revolution had taken place. The Act of Succession of 1534 called dissenters traitors: an oath was demanded. More refused. Such high-level dissent was intolerable to the new regime. He was sent to the Tower, and cross-examined by former colleagues. His core principle was that religious matters cannot be settled by royal whim. What's the point of theology, if the king can contradict it when it suits him? In a sense, his 'stand' resembled Luther's at the Diet of Worms fifteen years earlier. For both men, religious truth cannot be determined by an institution flexing its muscles: conscience must object to the claim. Finally, condemned, More spoke out. He declared that the Act of Supremacy was 'directly repugnant to the laws of God and his Holy Church, the supreme Government of which, or of any part whereof, may no temporal prince presume by any law to take upon him, as rightfully belonging to the See of Rome . . .'[2]

Archbishop Cranmer was proving to be a very effective holy henchman. Unlike his master, he sincerely believed in the Reformation, and even in the principle of royal supremacy. In 1540 he led a doctrinal committee, an attempt to justify the new regime on theological grounds. He declared that the Christian Church was naturally subject to temporal authority: God had delivered to 'all Christian princes . . . the whole cure of all their subjects, as well concerning the administration of God's word for the cure of souls, as concerning the ministration of things political and civil governance.'[3] According to this logic, the early church was less than a true Christian church, because it lacked political direction. Quite so, said Cranmer. The apostles of the first century had lacked 'remedy then for the correction of vice, or appointing of ministers', relying merely on 'the consent of Christian multitude among themselves'.[4] The Church needs to be politically controlled in order to be truly itself (an idea that still exists within Anglicanism). Cranmer's recent biographer, Diarmaid MacCulloch, draws attention to the strangeness of this position to most modern ears: 'Nowhere today can one find such a theory of royal supremacy in the Christian world. His premise about the divine ordering of society through Christian princes is diametrically opposed to the Western Church's post-1789 agonizing about its links with the State.'[5] Yet, regardless of 'agonizing', this remains the logical foundation of the Church of England, for as long as it is established.

For the rest of his reign, Henry carefully consolidated his new powers. He had excised papal authority from national life, by means of the new theology. But he didn't want an evangelical revolution; he remained suspicious of Luther and Tyndale. He would have liked to see Catholicism without the pope, were that possible. Was it possible? England's Church has laboured for centuries to keep the fantasy alive. His young son, Edward VI, was more sincere in his evangelical enthusiasm. Consequently, Cranmer had a freer hand to reform the religious life of the nation. His seven-year reign was a religious revolution, partly thanks to exiles from the Continental Reformation, who imported a style of humourless efficiency. Yet conservative forces were not entirely quashed: the reform still had to proceed with care, lest it provoke a reaction. The Prayer Book of 1552 was Cranmer's greatest achievement; it soon came to be seen as the definitive essence of this new Church. It replaced the theatre of Roman worship with the sober melodies of English prose.

In the short term, Cranmer's reforms suffered the reverse of Mary's reign. Cranmer was condemned and forced to rethink his entire theology. His belief in royal supremacy suddenly became a logical nightmare, for the new monarch denied it, and reinstated the pope. In the Tower he held to the principle that the monarch was the local ruler of the universal Christian Church, and that the pope was an impostor. 'Then what say you by Nero?' asked his accuser. 'He was the mightiest prince of the earth after Christ was ascended: was he head of Christ's Church?'[6] Cranmer had to admit that he was: he had been forced to swallow his own logic. Suddenly, royal supremacy made neither theological nor political sense. He had moved his allegiance from pope to monarch, and was now being punished for this – by the monarch.

The predicaments of More and Cranmer reveal that there was no logical position available during these years. Both positions share the same presupposition: that political and religious authority must harmonise, that each needs the other. When this harmony crumbles there is no logically coherent position to occupy. To see the king as subject to the pope, as More did, becomes nonsensical, if the king refuses to see himself in that way. And to see the king as the head of the Church, as Cranmer did, also becomes nonsensical if the king, or queen, doesn't play along.

Elizabeth was her father's daughter: unlike her siblings, she didn't let religion get in the way of a religious policy. She reverted to Cranmer's vision of the Church, as set out in his Prayer Book, but in her hands this vision was more conservative than reforming. The great task was to create consensus after the years of upheaval; and this meant suppressing radical reformers as well as Catholics.

Like her father, Elizabeth needed a third way, beyond Roman Catholicism and radical reform. It lay in herself, and in the ideal of the nation. A cult of the monarch had the power to appeal to both sides: traditionalists were attracted to the pseudo-papal pageantry and to the promise of order; reformers were attracted to the ideal of the strong Protestant nation. Thus emerged the myth of England's religious destiny: England as Israel. It helped, for a while, to defuse the religious argument. The defeat of the Spanish Armada had the unifying power of a World Cup match today. As long as it contributed to national unity, the Church was allowed to contain diverse views within itself. This is the origin of Anglicanism's famous tolerance, broadness, reasonability. It is important that we recognise that these virtues are rooted in establishment. To some, this is a good argument for establishment. To others, it is cause to suspect these virtues.

In the short run, the Elizabethan emphasis on Protestant nationalism was a force for unity. In the long run, it simply raised the stakes. It gave rise to a new breed of English reformer, whose faith coincided with a political project: to create a godly nation, on biblical lines. Puritanism was born at the Elizabethan court, from the marriage of nationalism and Protestant vocation. Its extreme form emerged in reaction to the apostasy of the Stuart court.

In the meantime, the dominant theology was one of Erastian order. Jewel, Whitgift and Bancroft continued the project of Cranmer: to justify the royal supremacy against both radical and papist. The most famous intellectual justification came from Richard Hooker, in *Of the Laws of Ecclesiastical Polity*. It held that Church and state were both divinely ordained, as was their unity. A unified body politic called for a Church that understood itself within the framework of the state. This did not make the Church subject to the whim of a monarch: in theory, power was shared among the various organs of the state, including Parliament, and harmony would prevail. Hooker's vision was of a Church that was, in effect, synonymous with the state: the other side of the same coin. The Church was the nation in its spiritual aspect, or the nation at prayer. This vision of a religious and political monoculture broke down in the nineteenth century, as we shall see. Yet no coherent new theory replaced it; Anglicanism found no new basis. It still relied, and relies, on the very threadbare rhetoric of national religious unity. For example, William Temple called the Church 'the whole people of England in its religious capacity'.[7] The Church of England remains founded on the ghost of Hooker's theory.

With the succession of James I, it was quickly apparent that the Elizabethan settlement lacked stability. Radical reformers were multiplying like rabbits, largely thanks to the press, which megaphoned their strident sermons. In 1603 the evangelical clergy presented James with a petition, allegedly representing a thousand of them. It was a profession of loyalty that veiled a threat: either us, or presbyterianism. From the king's point of view, it was only thanks to royal power that the evangelicals had any freedom from Rome – they should be quietly grateful. This was the dangerous consequence of the English Reformation: it had boosted the pride of both the monarchy and the reformers.

The government of Charles and Archbishop Laud was steeped in a conservative religious sensibility. It invested royalty with sacramental pathos, and it also invested episcopacy – the authority of the bishops – with greater weight than ever. To the Puritans, this version of Anglicanism seemed indistinguishable from Roman Catholicism, and they suspected Charles of wanting to do a Mary: to go back on the Reformation entirely. This was not mere paranoia: the court flirted with a return to Catholicism. Charles even married a Catholic.

In the 1620s and 1630s, the Puritans were the opposition: righteous, modern, vocal, and well organised (like the Labour Party in the mid 1990s). The king was seen as a new pope, which meant that a new 'break' was needed. He was also cast as Pharaoh, blocking the liberty of the people. England was Israel; its Church must be purged of idolatry – which included its episcopal system. The authority of the bishops became the key issue. Milton said that episcopacy forced him out of the Church; he had been 'church-outed by the prelates'. Of course the issue was political as well as religious: the bishops were the agents of royal supremacy, as well as reminders of Catholic error. Adrian Hastings comments, 'Most of the 16th century reformers preferred to abolish the episcopate as a medieval aberration. Where it survived within a Protestant church, most notably in England and Sweden, it was chiefly because the sovereign thought it easier to control the church with bishops than without them.'[8]

What did the Puritans want instead? It is easier to say what they opposed than what they proposed – rather like today's 'anti-capitalists'. Of course, they wanted a national Church that was unambiguously reformed. But there was a new account emerging every day of what a reformed Church ought to look like. Puritanism exalted individual conscience – a supremely fissiparous principle, leading to the multiplication of sects. Because they were persecuted, they naturally exalted the principle of toleration. This is one of the most complex areas in intellectual history: the relationship between Puritanism and early ideas of freedom, even of a secular society. A wholly new sort of radicalism was emerging that combined the religious zeal of Luther with the political zeal of Thomas Paine.

This politically progressive Puritanism was embodied in Milton. He was full of the Puritan national ideal. God had chosen England to be the leading Protestant nation, and England must react to its calling. He was also full of the rhetoric of toleration and liberty, and sincerely so.

Most religious zealots were at best ambiguous about liberty: if it stood in the way of godly reformation, it must go. Milton, perhaps more than anyone else, combined Reformation and humanist traditions: he was in the tradition of Erasmus and More as well as Luther and Calvin. He advocated religious freedom as a means to reformation. William Haller comments, 'Unworldly and inexperienced of men, he expected presbyterianism to usher in not theocracy but Utopia.'[9] If the state simply allowed free religious debate, the truth would out. The Church did not need the state's backing – indeed, that 'backing' always led to corruption. The state simply had to keep impartial order, while the truth won hearts and minds. Before anyone else was even able to understand the concept, Milton was advocating the separation of Church and state. His religious vision was streets ahead of Luther's or Calvin's: he saw, dimly, how reformed Christianity could interact with political modernity.

The main body of Puritans wanted to overthrow the episcopal system, or 'prelacy', and establish a form of Presbyterianism. This of course led to civil war and regicide. It has become axiomatic to us that revolutionary regimes are tyrannical. They have to consolidate their power, at the expense of toleration. In the short run there was no room for the tolerant face of Puritanism. In the longer run, however, it was that tolerant face that triumphed, though in the process it lost touch with its religious roots. After the violence of the Civil War there was a huge reaction against extremism. One might even say that the religious character of the English was forged here, in their horror at the Civil War. From now on, religion had to contribute to peace, order, stability. There was need of a unified national Church that was conservative, tolerant, and deeply suspicious of theology. The long-term legacy of Puritanism was its secular by-product. Puritans transmuted into Whigs, far more concerned with political liberty than Christian faith.

It was not the Puritans but their opponents, the Caroline divines, who determined the future of Anglicanism. The blood of Charles and Laud was the seed of modern Anglicanism. This is most clearly evident in relation to episcopacy. Before the Civil War, episcopacy was a grey area: it was not seen as a mark of a true church, just a matter of practicality. The Puritans attacked the fudge: if episcopacy was not extirpated it would come to dominate and define this Church. (And perhaps they were right: 'apostolic succession' became the rallying cry of the anti-Protestant Oxford Movement.) When the Puritans lost control of the Church, episcopacy was reinstated with renewed force. This tied the Church closer to the person of the monarch. As James' famous warning 'No bishop, no king' attests, the two institutions were intertwined. Both represented authority from above, by divine right. In the 1640s the two fell together, with the executions of Archbishop Laud and Charles I. But when they rose again, they were more firmly united than ever. For the next century, the High Church party was dominant and no questioning of either bishop or king was tolerated. The losers of the Civil War were thus the long-term victors, at least in terms of ecclesiastical history.

With the Restoration, political establishment became essential to this Church in a way that is perhaps unique in religious history. For its episcopate had no grounding in a wider Church. Instead of Rome, it needed the monarch. The head of the Church of England was not simply the monarch, but the monarch dressed as the pope.

After the rejection of Puritan extremism, there was another task: the rejection of a monarchy that claimed divine right and flirted with Roman Catholicism. The restored Stuarts had to be deposed again, in the Glorious Revolution of 1688. Parliament organised the succession of the Protestant William of Orange, who was willing to accept a constitutionally restrained crown. These two events, Restoration and Revolution, constitute a dual purge of England's ideological excesses: Puritanism and divine-right-Catholicism. Both options were renounced, both bridges burned, in favour of a double oxymoron: episcopal Protestantism and a constitutional monarchy.

The Anglican settlement continued in a new key. The *via media* became a matter of supremely good taste. To be too Protestant or too Catholic was deemed crude, uncivilised, thick. Reason became a major ingredient of Anglican theology; in many cases the main ingredient (the origin of the Latitudinarian party). Now was the heyday of the rational-pragmatic defence of establishment. It was seen as a wonderful defence against 'enthusiasm', meaning irrational religious feeling. Whether inclined towards popish superstition or dissenting fanaticism, religious enthusiasm was disloyal, disorderly. It was pathologised, associated with madness. The official national religion, in contrast, existed to order or educate religious feeling, to channel it into a rational-social end: being a good citizen. The purpose of the Church was to guard against religious zeal in any other sense.

In a sense, the real roots of this anti-theological revolution lie in the thought of Thomas Hobbes. During the Civil War he had formulated a new secular theory of politics. A state needed to be united, in order to be peaceful. Religion had to be tightly controlled by the secular ruler. The theory of the supremacy of the state is continued in Enlightenment and Romantic thought, culminating in Hegel and his ugly children.

Though establishment was politically unassailable after the Restoration, it was hardly beyond criticism. Monarchs were not very satisfactory heads of the Church, as the Stuarts continued to prove. Foreign Protestants had to be imported: William and Mary were Dutch Calvinists, and the Hanoverians were German Lutherans. The union with Scotland in 1707 created the most obvious religious anomaly of all: the established Church north of the border was, and is, Presbyterian rather than Anglican.

During the eighteenth century, English society became increasingly secular. Religion was valued for its social benefits, and the Church was happy to collude in this process. The key reaction was Methodism; its emotional ('enthusiastic') form of faith was widely seen as proving the necessity of an established Church, to maintain discipline and reasonability in religion; a sense of proportion. Many saw the later Evangelical revival within the Church in the same way. Both Methodism and Evangelicalism were returns of Puritanism, but politically castrated. Or, to be a little more precise, they were divorced from the political Enlightenment which, after a period of ambiguity (Milton and Locke), had become essentially anti-religious.

The eighteenth century was the golden age of the established Church. It became tightly woven into the political fabric of the nation, partly due to the immense amount of property it owned. While England's economy was still predominantly rural, the Church remained unassailable. A. N. Wilson writes:

> The squires in pre-industrial England were the

effectual administrators of the country. Their lands provided employment for the agricultural labourers who made up the bulk of the population. Their pew in the parish church signified the indissoluble union between Church and state at a local level, just as their patronage of the living demonstrated in concrete form the Erastian character of that Church.[10]

The Church also profited from an abiding popular fear of Roman Catholicism, and the emergence of a bullish national identity that was beginning to enjoy imperial adventures.

On the other hand, of course, the Enlightenment was hardly the Church's ally. The American colonies were proving the point: rational politics precluded this medieval hangover. In the 1780s, between the American and French revolutions, it must have seemed to a modern-minded observer that England was on the cusp of major constitutional change. Though it retained its traditional religious structures, its trajectory was patently secular: surely it would pursue political enlightenment and become a secular republic, along American lines. Then the French messed everything up. In reaction to the secular excesses of their Revolution, the notion of political enlightenment changed course suddenly and violently. It began to seem more enlightened to be cautiously conservative. Alec Vidler comments, 'The effect of the French Revolution in England was therefore to strengthen the forces of conservatism, and to set the clock back. Had it not been for this reaction, parliament might have been reformed, the dissenters, Catholic and Protestant, freed from their disabilities, and the slave trade abolished a generation earlier than they were.'[11]

Burke was the herald of this new era; his romantic conservatism gave the established Church a massive new lease of intellectual life. The value of religion lay in its contribution to political stability. Burke, who had no interest in theology, was the representative Anglican of the period. And of course he was the archetypal Tory (though a Liberal). His pragmatism towards the Church was followed by Disraeli, Churchill and others. It is important to be very clear on this point: such pragmatism is theologically indefensible. To advocate a form of Christianity because it is politically useful is to make the Gospel subservient to a secular end. Tory Anglicanism is constantly in grave danger of committing this very serious heresy.

Coleridge, better known as a Romantic poet, was also one of the key Anglican thinkers of the nineteenth century. In his youth, the French Revolution had tempted him towards chiliastic fantasies. He resisted them and, like Wordsworth, became essentially a Burkean. He knew that Burke was in tune with the drift of Continental thought: the Romantic nationalism of Herder and Hegel. Under the influence of these thinkers, he renounced the Romantic individualism of his youth, which now seemed to lead in the direction of Shelley's atheism. 'My fixed principle is: that a Christianity without a Church exercising spiritual authority is vanity and dissolution.'[12] Romanticism had turned against the tenets of the political Enlightenment.

On the Constitution of the Church and State appeared in 1830. It argues that the Church of England must be considered from two perspectives at once. On one hand it is the National Church, on the other hand it is part of the universal Christian Church. A National Church of some sort is a political necessity: it mediates culture and education through a learned caste, a 'clerisy'. Without this regulation of culture there would be anarchy. So far, Coleridge is talking as a political scientist; proposing a model for all states, whether Christian or not. It is an ideal influenced by Hegel: a state needs cultural unity, and that means religious unity. 'Religion, true or false, is and ever has been the centre of gravity in a realm, to which all other things must and will accommodate themselves',[13] wrote Coleridge. The supreme form of state religion is an established Protestant Church, for it is self-contained: it does not entail allegiance to an external authority, i.e. the pope. (The influence of Hobbes is notable here.) Such a state enables intellectual and political freedom, as far as these things are compatible with order. 'Among the numerous blessings of the English Constitution, the introduction of an Established Church makes an especial claim on the gratitude of scholars and philosophers; in England, at least, where the principles of Protestantism have conspired with the freedom of the government to double all its salutary powers by the removal of its abuses.'[14]

Protestant establishment has produced an unprecedentedly healthy body politic, Coleridge says. This is open to question, of course: many of his contemporaries would have denied that political liberty is dependent on established religion, or on religion at all. The point is that Coleridge falls into the classic modern trap: he justifies the Church on political grounds. This is bad ecclesiology because the case becomes gradually weaker as political culture develops in a secular direction – to see the Church as the lynchpin of the state becomes increasingly unfeasible. And of course this is what has gradually happened. Coleridge would have done a greater service to the

Church if he had tried to justify it independently of its
constitutional function.

In fact, Coleridge's thesis was already somewhat reactionary and nostalgic. The idea of a single national
religious culture had begun its long terminal decline. In
1828 the Test Act was repealed, which meant that Dissenters could hold public office. In 1829 Catholic
Emancipation restored political rights to the most feared
branch of dissenters. Vidler comments:

> The combined effect of the repeal of the Test Act
> and of Catholic Emancipation was to deal its death-
> blow to the old ideal, canonized by Hooker in his
> Ecclesiastical Policy, that Church and State in
> England were one society. The ideal had never been
> completely realized, and it has by now worn very
> thin. But so long as only members of the Church of
> England could sit in parliament, it seemed *in principle*
> to be maintained. In 1830 it was manifestly an anach-
> ronism.[15]

Catholic Emancipation was a severe shock to national
identity. Britain had built its identity, bloodily, by choosing
to be Protestant rather than Catholic. In effect it had
suffered a civil war lasting well over a century, beginning
with Henry VIII and ending with the Glorious Revolution
in 1688. It had settled its internal crisis by opting for
Protestantism. Why was it now jeopardising that hard-
won settlement, by inviting Catholics back into public
life? To many people, Catholic Emancipation looked like
cultural suicide.

Yet Protestant nationalists could take heart from
Britain's ever-increasing imperial role. Surely this was
proof that her religious nationalism was indeed God-

ordained? Yet foreign success raised plenty of anomalies. In
1794 the British had annexed Corsica, and had maintained
Catholicism as its official religion. Did Britain's commitment to Protestantism only obtain at home? Also, it was
beginning to acquire an empire in the East: was it to
declare that millions of subject Hindus and Muslims in
India were officially Anglican?

But of course the real logical problem was closer to
home. Ireland was an intolerable affront to English, and
Anglican, identity. It exposed that identity as a sham. If
Britain really believed in itself as a great Protestant nation,
why did it tolerate Ireland's Catholicism? And if Ireland
was allowed its own religious identity, why not political
also? The problem would dominate nineteenth-century
politics – and theology as well.

The Church's response to the new political landscape
could not have been more equivocal. It rose to the challenge by delving deep into its rich history of disunity.

After the Civil War, the argument between Catholic
and Protestant had been settled, at least superficially.
Though Protestant, this Church rejected radical Protestantism: its episcopacy was the sign of this. Paul Avis
says, 'In Anglicanism before the Oxford Movement there
was little sense that it might be necessary to choose
between a high view of the sacraments and episcopacy,
on the one hand, and the principles of the Reformation,
on the other.'[16] But now, because establishment looked
vulnerable, there was a need to think about theology
again. The term 'Anglicanism' was coined in the 1830s –
a sign of the new religious self-consciousness.

Tractarianism, also known as the Oxford Movement,
began in 1833. A group of conservative Oxford dons
accused the Whig government of ecclesiastical cynicism.

'National Apostasy' was the founding tract, based on Keble's sermon of July 1833. The government had appeased the Irish by withdrawing a number of Anglican bishoprics from Ireland. Did the government not realise that those bishoprics were put there by God? The Church had to remember that it was a divine institution, said Keble. 'What answer can we make henceforth to the partisans of the bishop of Rome, when they taunt us with being a mere Parliament Church?'[17] It is like a teenager realising that his mother is not a virgin.

The dignity of the Church could only be defended along Catholic lines: 'apostolic succession' was exalted as the essence of the Church. The sacramental life of the Church was rediscovered: all sorts of rather dusty doctrines and rites were suddenly reinvested with new meaning. This sacramental emphasis was perfectly acceptable within Anglicanism, as long as it knew its place. But the Tractarians broke the rules; they called the Reformers crude heretics, ignorant of the grandeur of the Church. They said that Protestantism naturally led to vacuous rationalism, and subservience to a godless state. The Church had become, in Newman's phrase, 'a department of government'. This is what caused Manning to leave the Church: 'Erastianism was hateful to me. The Royal Supremacy was, in my mind, an invasion of the Headship of our Lord.'[18]

John Henry Newman was the John Lennon of the movement. He believed in it with an intensity that led him to go beyond it, to betray it, to transcend it. His *Apologia Pro Vita Sua* is an account of his spiritual journey, from the safety of its Roman conclusion. The book's title embodies the paradox of this man: classical stiffness masking Romantic egotism. As a young man Newman found himself the sworn opponent of 'liberalism', rather like T. S. Eliot a century later. In fact he tried to limit his anti-liberalism to theology — 'by liberalism I mean liberalism in *religion*'[19] — but of course religious conservatism entails political conservatism. The Church could only be rescued by a rediscovery of its innate authority; it had to recapture the assurance it had possessed in the seventeenth century, when it dominated the political sphere, rather than being dominated by it.

He did not want disestablishment; indeed he feared it, very much. This is evident in a tract called 'Thoughts on the Ministerial Commission'. He asks, how will the Church live unless the government respects and protects it?

> We know how miserable is the state of religious bodies not supported by the State. Look at the Dissenters on all sides of you, and you will see at once that their Ministers, depending simply upon the people, become the *creatures* of the people. Are you content that this should be your case? Alas! Can a greater evil befall Christians, than for their teachers to be guided by them instead of guiding? . . . Is it not our very office to *oppose* the world? Can we then allow ourselves to *court* it? To preach smooth things and prophesy deceits? To make the way of life easy to the rich and indolent, and to bribe the humbler classes by excitements and strong intoxicating doctrine? Surely it must not be so; and the question recurs, on *what* are we to rest our authority, when the State deserts us?[20]

This is a clear glimpse into the muddled heart of Newman's thought. In order to oppose the world, the

Church must be established. This shows how firmly his conception of the Church is rooted in the Middle Ages, how deeply it fears modernity. His thought is ruled by fear.

When he later recounts his early career, his tone is precious, defensive. He regrets his attacks on Rome, almost on aesthetic grounds: 'I felt that my language had a vulgar and rhetorical look about it.'[21] The great crime of his old Church is that it made him untrue to himself – is there not a hint of Wildean self-regard here?

Though it was critical of Erastianism, the Oxford Movement never really questioned establishment. It was in love with an older ideal of establishment: Rome was therefore its logical conclusion. Avis comments, 'The men of the Oxford Movement . . . were politically, socially and theologically reactionary. They were profoundly unsympathetic to the Enlightenment with its challenges to all traditional and unassailable claims.'[22] The cult of the Oxford Movement, which has never really abated, attests to the sad difficulty that the Church of England has had with political modernity, its natural propensity to romantic (Rome-antic) nostalgia.

The Oxford Movement was largely a reaction to the rise of the Evangelicals. An elite group of Evangelicals wielded huge political power, like in the US today. They were very confident of their righteousness; they considered their influence on the British Empire to be all that redeemed it from mere tyranny. Their power within the Church was demonstrated in 1847, with the Gorham case. An Evangelical priest had defied his bishop and denied the doctrine of baptismal regeneration. The Evangelicals went to the secular courts to defend the priest, and won. Avis writes: 'This judgement at once undermined both the sacramental basis and the hierarchical structure of High Church ecclesiology: the conception of the Church as a visible divine society, distinct from the world and ruled by its bishops.'[23] The Tractarians saw this as proof that, under Protestant influence, Anglicanism was cravenly Erastian.

The ecclesiological tussle was only of interest to a minority. Other perspectives were emerging to which all this seemed nonsense on stilts. In 1845 Engels reported to Marx that 'all the writers of the bourgeoisie are unanimous on this point, that the workers are not religious, and do not attend church'. The 1851 census bore this out, more or less. It found that around half the population went to church, and that this figure was split between Anglicans and Nonconformists. And most disturbingly of all, it found that the urban masses were very largely unchurched.

The Church needed to overcome its inner rift and reconnect with the masses. The theologian F. D. Maurice tried to show the way. He was influenced by Coleridge's defence of the National Church, which opened him to Hegelianism also. Like Thomas Arnold, another Latitudinarian, he realised that the middle way must be repaired after the ravages of Tractarianism. As he saw it, the Church's pan-national role committed it to taking socialism seriously, which was at that time identified with the Chartist movement. With his friend Ludlow he called for the Church's conversion to socialism. Maurice was the founder of the Anglican Left. It is a strange thing, the Anglican Left: it is genuinely radical in its politics, yet amazingly accepting of establishment. It believes that establishment ought to work to its advantage, and persists in this belief despite all the evidence (rather like the woman who believes she can change her no-good man). This seeming contradiction, between socialism and acceptance of the *status quo*, is largely down to Maurice. He developed an 'incarnational' theology that sought to emphasise the basic goodness of the created world and the social order, which belonged within 'the Kingdom of Christ'. Today this sounds intensely conservative, in its affirmation of the family and the nation, but it also inspired the 'social gospel' that was subsequently developed by Anglo-Catholics.

If there is one man who embodies the transition from Victorian to contemporary Anglicanism, it is Gladstone. In 1839, as a young MP, he wrote a book entitled *The State in its Relations to the Church*. It was an earnest defence of the national Church, including its controversial role in Ireland. Gladstone's Anglicanism was strongly inspired by the national ideal: Britain's religious unity was key to her role as world saviour. The great virtue of an established Church was that it could accommodate everyone, even 'those who attend Christian ordinances only in compliance with human opinion; and those who see nothing in Christianity but a system of outward forms, in an establishment nothing but a method of preserving social order and of repressing religious extravagance'.[24] This is oddly honest: an admission that the Church is attractive because it is not too religious.

Elsewhere he insisted on the superiority of Anglicanism to any Dissenting church, due to its comprehensiveness, its tranquillity, its sobriety.

> But, further, her spirit is so much more catholic; her system affords so much less scope for the pride of self-will; her privileges, avowedly open to all,

come to men so much less as favoured *individuals*,
so much more as members of a favoured body,
and that body the universal Church, in which our
individuality is as it were absorbed. All these things
seem to me in our communion so much to hinder
and shame presumption, and so loudly and clearly
to preach humility, that I cannot but feel persuaded
the Establishment, *even* as it is at present, affords far
more efficient instrumental aids for entering
thoroughly into the mind and spirit of the Redeemer,
than rival schools of more plausible pretension.[25]

The national Church is like a wonderful public school open
to all, with beautiful playing-fields and mild-mannered
teachers: the alternatives are like nasty little back-street
establishments with too many rules. Yet it is important
that we do not dismiss Gladstone's argument too quickly,
for in a sense this is the essence of the pro-establishment
case. This Church can offer a uniquely rounded form of
Christianity. It is a wonderful synthesis of Protestant and
Catholic; it is open to rationality, the arts, history, society;
it values order and holiness; it weeds out demagogues and
charlatans. Surely it is the best of all possible churches –
if only you discount the fact of its reliance upon the state. Is
not the theological anomaly a price worth paying, for all
the benefits? Many other defenders of establishment seem
to do this little deal in their minds, like pious Fausts.

Famously, Gladstone changed his mind on the Anglican
presence in Ireland: he came to power in 1868 promising
to disestablish the Church there – a policy effected in
1871 (which led to his espousal of Home Rule). Philip
Magnus comments, 'He reached the premiership by way
of a furious assault upon the Irish Church establishment

which he had once conceived it to be his most sacred duty to seek to preserve unimpaired at any cost.'[26] He also prepared the way for the disestablishment of the Church in Wales. Yet he remained a fervent Anglican all his life. In a sense he was the first really modern defender of establishment: he realised that it had to be flexible in order to survive, and also that it had to emphasise its social benefits. Like Maurice, he wanted to reunite and strengthen Anglicanism by modernising it. This meant, above all, modernising the national ideal. (Incidentally, Tony Blair compares very interestingly with Gladstone: another reforming Anglican patriot who can only keep alive the old ideal by modernising it almost out of existence.)

The famous Victorian crisis of faith did not do the established Church much harm. Indeed an established Church is attractive to post-Christian humanists. Perhaps the best evidence of this comes from the two greatest novelists of the time, Dickens and Eliot.

Dickens was not interested in theology, except to assert a humanist Christianity against more dogmatic forms. His religious piety coincides with his social concern. The centrepiece of his Christianity is Christmas, understood as the union of charity and conviviality. He is a harsh critic of any religion that lacks these two things. He finds dogmatic Christianity both ridiculous and sinister: Chadband etc. One of his most psychologically realistic heroes, *Little Dorrit*'s Arthur Clenham, is in revolt against his native Calvinism. All of Dickens' heroes and heroines adhere to a religion based on the imitation of Christ (the depictions make little attempt at psychological realism). Dickens often posed as a Christian reformer, despite his indifference to theology. He often upbraided the Church for peddling irrelevant theology and losing sight of 'the example of Jesus'.

George Eliot is the modern novelist *par excellence*; she invests more pathos, more seriousness in the novel than any predecessor. She, more than anyone, severs the form's connection to flippancy. Her career as a novelist arises from her critique of religion. She was an Evangelical until she moved on to literature, investing her writing with deep secular-evangelistic purpose. (She was much hated by Nietzsche for her Christian-based humanism.) Her first book, *Scenes of Clerical Life* (1857), consists of three stories about rural parishes. One concerns an Evangelical pastor called Mr Tryan. Though a do-gooder, he does good. But his reforms meet much resistance, and he gets depressed. Here Eliot steps in with one of her little authorial asides:

> It is apt to be so in this life, I think. While we are coldly discussing a man's career, sneering at his mistakes, blaming his rashness, and labelling his opinions – 'he is Evangelical and narrow', or 'Latitudinarian and Pantheistic', or 'Anglican and supercilious' – that man, in his solitude, is perhaps shedding hot tears because his sacrifice is a hard one, because strength and patience are failing him to speak the difficult word, and do the difficult deed.[27]

This is a neat example of Eliot's post-religiosity. The human story constitutes a perspective over and above the various religious perspectives. Elsewhere she sums up the effect of the town's religious reformation. Though it had made some people into prigs (women especially), it had also spread among the people 'that idea of duty, that recognition of something to be lived for beyond the mere satisfaction of self, which is to the moral life what

the addition of a great central ganglion is to animal life'.[28]
Does one not begin to sympathise with Nietzsche? This
woman really thinks she has understood religion; its part
in humanity's evolution. She assumes a similar position of
superiority to the other two vicars in the book. Frankly,
her attitude to the Church is patronising. It does a great
deal of good, its ministers mean well. But it goes without
saying that there is no intellectual charisma of the higher
level, such as an artist might possess.

I digress somewhat. My point is that Eliot sentimental-
ises the Church. It is a charming feature of traditional
communities, part of the life of the common people. This
sub-theological pastoral is also present in many other
writers of the period, from Wordsworth to Hardy.

This mood of para-Christian humanism that Dickens
and Eliot both exemplify is likely to be well disposed
towards the established Church. For an established Church
is intrinsically committed to 'the social gospel', and to
the unifying of society. And it tends to put its social
mission before doctrinal rigidity and puritanical exclusi-
vity. This is really the secret of establishment's persistence:
to weakly Christian liberals, which is most of the ruling
class and intelligentsia since about 1700, the Church of
England is infinitely preferable to any religious alternative.
And it is instinctively felt that its abolition would lead
to unpalatable alternatives. (American Evangelicalism is
obviously the present threat – Dickens, incidentally, was
an influential critic of it.)

The sympathy of the post-Christian intelligentsia
towards the established Church did not continue into the
twentieth century. Let us offend every literary expert and
suggest that the early twentieth-century equivalents of
Dickens and Eliot were Lawrence and Woolf. The

Victorian pair preserved a strict politeness towards the Church, rooted in an assumption of its benign social effect. The Edwardian pair could not uphold this attitude; it reeked of hypocrisy (Lawrence was raised a Nonconformist, which obviously affects his view of the established Church). Literary Modernism entailed a new sort of iconoclastic honesty, for which we should, perhaps, thank Nietzsche.

Although, as we have seen, Anglican hegemony had been theoretically undermined by 1830, it took a long time to crumble. Non-Anglicans were still widely perceived to be unpatriotic. Gradually this changed, partly thanks to Gladstone. His Liberal Party worked hard to secure equality for non-Anglicans – it abolished compulsory church rates and the application of religious tests at Oxford and Cambridge. The education Act of 1870 allowed non-Anglican state-aided education (criticised by die-hard Protestants as 'Rome on the rates').

Of course, many Nonconformists called for total equality and disestablishment of the Church of England. The Liberation Society had been founded in mid-century: Edward Miall was the Peter Tatchell of the cause, tirelessly exposing establishment abuses. But of course Gladstone's reforms did much to defuse calls for disestablishment. He made radical campaigners for disestablishment seem shrill and excessive; he seriously stole their fire. He was helped in this by the resurgence of 'papal aggression', when the pope declared his infallibility in 1870. By reacting indignantly, he seemed to speak for all Protestants. The Dissenters were still not convinced, of course. At the turn of the century the Congregationalist theologian P. T. Forsyth called Anglicanism 'that great, godly, and unfortunate Church . . . [bringing] in its train the torpor, neglect, and corruption of monopoly.'[29] He also made the powerful observation that the state had secularised the Church more than the Church had spiritualised the state. The Methodist leader Hugh Price Hughes similarly reasserted the principle of ecclesiastical freedom: 'It seems to us as monstrous that the State should domineer over the Church as that the Church should domineer over the State . . . we can no more tolerate the interference of the secular power than could the Popes of the Middle Ages.'[30]

At the beginning of the twentieth century the Church was looking rather vulnerable. Attendance figures had begun to dip – partly due to the demise of the old squirearchy, partly due to the spread of fashionable atheism. In 1914 Parliament voted to disestablish the Church in Wales, which was put into effect after the War. (The Archbishop of Canterbury, Davidson, had opposed it.) The established Church was now only established in England, not Scotland, Ireland or Wales. This made a nonsense of its control by Parliament, which obviously contained many people from these establishment-free provinces. Before, the justification was that Parliament was composed of lay members of the Church: this was not strictly the case after 1830, but remained feasible enough for a while. But in 1906 the new government was mostly non-Anglican. Asquith and Lloyd George were both secularised Nonconformists, with power to appoint Anglican bishops. Tory politicians tended to be nominally Anglican but effectively secular: 'There was hardly a straightforward Christian believer in the front rank of politics in these years', says Adrian Hastings.[31] Throughout almost all of the twentieth century the Church was controlled by an overwhelmingly non-Anglican Parliament.

The First World War was a bad advertisement for

European Christianity in general, and the Church of England in particular. In 1914 Dr Winnington-Ingram, the Bishop of London, played the role of a clerical recruiting sergeant. He proudly posed wearing a uniform over his dog-collar. He said, 'I think the Church can best help the nation first of all by making it realise that it is engaged in a Holy War, and not be afraid of saying so. Christ died on Good Friday for Freedom, Honour and Chivalry, and our boys are dying for the same things.'[32] Haig's Christianity was even more terrifying. Clifford Longley comments: 'it seems likely that only a man who was certain he had God on his side could have gone on ordering thousands of soldiers to their deaths, day after day.'[33] It is a cliché of modern history, but may as well be repeated: the shock of the First World War left all traditional structures shaky. 'The established church was part of the old order, rural, aristocratic, hierarchical, which was smashed to pieces at the Battle of the Somme on 1 July 1916', writes Peter Hitchens.[34]

Soon after the War, William Temple emerged as the great hope of the Church. He could hardly have been a more establishment figure; his father was archbishop of Canterbury. But he was an establishment reformer, like Gladstone; he did much to bring Anglican theology up to date with its changing context.

In 1917 he founded the Life and Liberty Movement, which demanded spiritual freedom for the Church. 'If the Church is to have new life, even if it is to maintain the life which it has, it must have liberty, even at the cost, if necessary, of disestablishment.'[35] It was an important development that a loyal Anglican was even willing to use the word. 'Our movement is not aiming at Disestablishment; it aims at self-government for the Church. Many of us, including myself, would infinitely prefer to secure that end by some other means than Disestablishment . . . But we feel the need of self-government to be so vital that we are prepared to face even Disestablishment if self-government can be obtained in no other way.'[36] Tough talk: rather like a teenager threatening to divorce his parents.

The General Strike of 1926 showed that the Church was split on economic thought. Most of the bishops were Tories, but Temple led the reforming, mildly socialist party. He chaired a conference calling for redistribution of wealth. Baldwin replied that the churches had no more business trying to settle the coal dispute than the Federation of British Industry had to revise the Athanasian Creed.

Temple went on to become the archetypal new establishmentarian: liberal, mildly socialist, globally conscious, ecumenical, yet still keenly patriotic. He was a founder of the World Council of Churches, and a key architect of the welfare state. Yet his vision was essentially Edwardian in its reliance on the public-school ethos and Christian nationalism. Kent comments, 'He dreamed of reidentifying church and nation, and of making the Anglican church in its turn the centre of a worldwide Christian unity.'[37] Though an impeccable liberal, Temple felt no need to downplay his pride in the national tradition. (Since the Second World War, liberalism and nationalism have not sat together so easily.) He wrote:

> Whether logical or not, the English method has always been to enjoy all kinds of excellence together as far as possible, retaining the glamour and unifying influence of monarchy with the steadying influence

of hereditary aristocracy while welcoming the progressive impetus of democracy . . . The church of
England, like other Churches, has often failed to be
completely Christian – always, indeed, if we take
those words in all their proper depth of meaning;
but it has never failed to be utterly, completely,
provokingly, adorably English.[38]

In 1919, partly thanks to Temple's efforts, the Enabling
Act had set up the Church Assembly, a precursor of
the General Synod. This smoothed the path of Church
legislation, which would now be passed by the Crown as
a matter of course. But eight years later this gentle drift
to autonomy was rudely interrupted.

The Prayer Book crisis was of course rooted in the
Church's internal rift, which was as bitter as ever. The
Anglo-Catholics and Evangelicals fought like angry siblings. Their disputes were straight out of the sixteenth
century: the length of vestments, praying for the dead,
and so on. One of the main issues was 'the reservation
of the sacrament': should priests be allowed to imitate
the Roman practice of putting aside consecrated left-overs
in a special little cupboard? One could try to explain all
this by looking for the underlying theological issues, but
perhaps the best way of putting it is that the Anglo-
Catholics and Evangelicals had totally incompatible styles.
The former seemed arrogant, effeminate, obscurantist;
the latter seemed prosaic, aggressive, banal. Maybe all
modern Christians to some extent resent their religion:
in the case of Anglicans it couldn't be easier.

In 1927 a mildly revised version of the Prayer Book
was agreed by the bishops, and sent to Parliament for
ratification. And refused. The main reason was that Evan-

gelical MPs, led by Sir William Joynson-Hicks, the Home Secretary, sensed Anglo-Catholic bias. The bishops were reeling in anger for a few years, and disestablishment was much talked of. If the bishops were not allowed to control the way the Church worshipped, what was their authority for?

The bishops soon got over the humiliation of 1927. All except one. Until this point Hensley Henson, Bishop of Durham, had been an establishment man of the old school. He had criticised Temple's flirtation with disestablishment and socialism. He was among the most likely candidates to replace Davidson as archbishop of Canterbury. He suddenly abandoned all diplomacy and chose principle before preferment. He denounced the 'Protestant underworld' that had fixed the bishops' defeat. And he came out for disestablishment, denouncing the Church's subjection to a secular state. Despite his aversion to the Evangelicals, he was not really an Anglo-Catholic either; he cursed both their houses. He was an old-fashioned 'middle way' man. But now he realised that the middle way was intolerably dependent on establishment, which he could not defend. He could only be a sign of contradiction, of protest. Owen Chadwick comments:

> For the rest of his time as a bishop he could hardly make a speech without a reference to the need for disestablishment if the Church was to be healthy. Any ill which he saw, like a ritual brawl in Marazion in Cornwall, he fancied could be mended by disestablishment. But he knew himself to be a *lone wolf*.[39]

Let us declare Hensley Henson the hero of this brief historical survey. He renounced the warm club of establishment and embodied the loneliness of Anglicanism, its lack of a place to lay its head. But, lest we seem to romanticise isolation, let us refer back to Chapter One and include Michael Ramsey as well in this brief prize-giving. 'I've never been plain C of E like Fisher,' he said in retirement. 'I've been partly nonconformist and partly Tractarian. I never cared much for establishments.'[40] He helped Anglicanism to begin to understand itself away from its established status; to withdraw heart and soul from the attachment. Indeed, with Ramsey the Church was learning to use establishment rather than be used by it. Partly due to his influence upon many leading Anglicans, including Runcie, and now Williams, he enabled the demise of the Church of England to be fruitfully slow, rich in softly-spoken Christian cunning.

Chapter Three

RECENT APOLOGISTS

I N T H I S C H A P T E R I look at eleven defences of establishment, mostly very recent. There are obviously twenty
others I might have picked, but this selection is intended to
suggest the range of pro-establishment argument. Finally
I inquire into the present Archbishop of Canterbury's
position.

Defenders of establishment fall into two categories: the
Stoic and the Defiant. The Stoic realises the game is up,
more or less, but sees his Christian duty as staying put;
the Defiant denies it.

Eliot

T. S. Eliot is the archetypal Anglo-Catholic traditionalist.
It is interesting that he was once American: his career
signifies a renunciation of the Enlightenment, a return to
an older idea of order. But by the twentieth century
such an ideal had to be reconstructed, in defiance of
modern political life. Such a stance can hardly avoid being
on nodding terms with fascism.

In 1927 he came out as a classicist in literature, an
Anglo-Catholic in religion, and a royalist in politics. After
this declaration his poetic output is minimal. Literary and

social criticism becomes his primary platform, or pulpit; the arena for a new voice of cultural authority. The limitations of literature are explained in *After Strange Gods*, published in 1933. The currently influential writers, such as Yeats and Lawrence, are all 'heretics', in that they undermine a common religious culture. They are ultimately on the side of 'liberalism', which is a force of decadence and disorder. Eliot considers his stance to be essentially religious: he is defending 'orthodoxy'. But of course this is also a reactionary political stance, sympathetic to the tradition of French counter-revolutionary thought. The root of his religious orthodoxy is an insistence upon man's fallen condition: 'I doubt whether what I am saying can convey very much to anyone for whom the doctrine of Original Sin is not a very real and tremendous thing.'[1] Notoriously, he states his belief that cultural health depends upon cultural and ethnic unity. 'The population should be homogenous; where two or more cultures exist in the same place they are likely either to be fiercely self-conscious or to become adulterate.'[2]

Eliot was provoked into writing *The Idea of a Christian Society* by 'the events of 1938': Europe's descent into neo-pagan horror. England faces a choice: Christianity or paganism. At present, society is dominated by Liberalism, which is seen as a temporary compromise-position. It will become a form of paganism, such as those that rage in Germany and Russia, unless we decide on the only alternative. 'If you will not have God (and he is a jealous God) you should pay your respects to Hitler or Stalin.'[3] Eliot partially distances his discourse from political reality; he plays Plato, sketching out a Christian society in idealised terms. The new model must not be an attempt to return to any past model, he says, which is difficult to take seriously. For he proceeds to sketch out an organic state, steeped in Hooker, Coleridge and medieval Christendom. Perhaps above all it is Hegelian, in its insistence that religion must be incarnated in the life of the people:

> The unitary community should be religious-social, and it must be one in which all classes, if you have classes, have their centre of interest . . . For the great majority of the people . . . religion must be primarily a matter of behaviour and habit, must be integrated with its social life, with its business and its pleasures; and the specifically religious emotions must be a kind of extension and sanctification of the domestic and social emotions.[4]

In such a culture, 'the dissentients must remain marginal, tending to make only marginal contributions'.[5]

Such a society will probably have an established church, he thinks. What is certain is that if a church is already established, its disestablishment would be disastrous:

> [T]he very act of disestablishment separates [a Church] more definitely and irrevocably from the life of the nation than if it had never been established. The effect on the mind of the people of the visible and dramatic withdrawal of the Church from the affairs of the nation, of the deliberate recognition of two standards and ways of life, of the Church's abandonment of all those who are not by their wholehearted profession within the fold – this is incalculable . . . It appears to assume something which I am not yet ready to take for granted: that the division between Christians and non-Christians

in this country is already, or is determined to become, so clear that it can be reduced to statistics.[6]

This sentiment is at the heart of the whole establishment debate. At the risk of being slightly provocative, all advocates of establishment are, like Eliot, nostalgic for Christendom. They want a situation in which religion is culturally natural, and its rejection is deviant. For 'you cannot have a national Christian society, a religious-social community, a society with a political philosophy founded upon the Christian faith, if it is constituted as a mere congeries of private and independent sects.'[7] What Eliot ultimately loathes and fears is the idea of people *choosing* about religion: choosing whether or not to be religious, choosing which religion to believe. This would entail 'that conflict between citizenship and church membership, between public and private morality, which today makes moral life so difficult for everyone, and which in turn provokes that craving for a simplified, monistic solution of statism or racism which the National Church can only combat if it recognises its position as a part of the Universal Church.'[8] In other words, our only defence against fascism is to repent of the Enlightenment and the Reformation. Eliot's claim to prophetic status was partly rooted in the sense that he had seen the future, in the form of the United States, and hated it. Eliot's theology is so deeply political that the following disclaimer rings rather hollow: 'What is worst of all is to advocate Christianity, not because it is true, but because it might be beneficial.'[9]

We should be grateful to Eliot in the same way that we should be grateful to Newman. He pointed out that if you really want to defend Anglicanism, applying unflinching intellectual honesty, you have to go down this

route. You have to reject liberalism, democracy, pluralism.
You have to revive the ideal of the Christian nation, and
indeed of Christendom, and denounce the Enlightenment.
We might abhor Eliot's conclusions, but we should admire
the intellectual honesty. In contrast, Temple was a flabby
thinker who cared more about sounding modern than
forging a coherent account of Anglican identity. With
hardly a single exception, official Anglican thought has
followed Temple's lead, and avoided Eliot's intellectual
honesty. But let us be honest about Eliot's vision. It is a
sort of Christian version of fascism, intended to stave off
the thing itself.

Lewis

C. S. Lewis was not a significant theorist of Church–state
relations. Yet he is very important to my theme. He shows
how establishment, in the wider sense of the involvement
of religion in the dominant culture, is very largely a
matter of style.

Lewis is a difficult phenomenon to untangle. His prose
is thoroughly dated: it conjures up a world where there
was a difference between a decent chap and a cad, and
'making love' meant gentle flirtation. Yet millions of
Christians, even today, look upon him as a saintly sage, a
doctor of the Church. Is it that his forceful defence of
Christianity transcends its cultural limitations, or is it that
Christians are nostalgic for those cultural limitations?

Born in Ulster, Lewis became an Oxford don. He
taught English Literature at a time when the humanities
were becoming decidedly secular. In consequence his
religious writing has a pervasive note of defiance. He was
not a theologian, except in an amateur sense. He did not

pay much attention to Continental theology, though the theological revolution associated with Barth was in full swing. This amateurism epitomises the intellectual ethos of Anglicanism: surely theology can be handled by a cultural all-rounder; surely common sense counts for more than Germanic cleverness? This attitude made Lewis feel that he was well enough equipped to speak for Christian England, which he began to do during the Second World War, via radio broadcasts. In 1940 Churchill had said of the Battle of Britain: 'Upon this battle depends the survival of Christian civilisation.' Lewis was fleshing this out.

Auden once categorised thinkers in terms of their desire either to create a New Jerusalem, or to regain a Lost Eden. Lewis was the ultimate Lost Eden man. In the spirit of wartime propaganda, he portrayed his country as an essentially homogenous Christian society. Of course, he had to admit that there were rival worldviews, but he gave the impression that these were marginal, rather cowardly affairs.

In reaction to his Ulster upbringing, he adopted a broad approach to Christianity, seeing its denominational differences as tragically unnecessary. He was thus naturally in tune with the 'middle way' appeal of Anglicanism. In the Preface to *Mere Christianity*, he announces that his approach is consciously non-denominational. Partly this is because he is not an expert in the finer points of theology that separate denominations, he says. 'And secondly, I think that we must admit that the discussion of these disputed points has no tendency at all to bring an outsider into the Christian fold.'[10]

His first chapter begins by attacking 'the view I call Christianity-and-water, the view which simply says there

is a good God in Heaven and everything is all right –
leaving out the difficult and terrible doctrines about sin
and hell and the devil, and the redemption.'[11] This is
typical Lewis rhetoric: bravely realistic, impatient with
evasion. But, in the light of the Preface, the rhetoric is
questionable. He himself is evading certain 'difficult and
terrible doctrines' – those questions of ecclesiastical
and political authority which are chiefly responsible for
inter-denominational strife. His own evasion, of course,
is presented as a virtue, in the present rhetorical context.
But in reality it leads to a falsely simplified version of
Christianity that evades ecclesiastical and political reality.

For Lewis, then, Christianity's relationship to politics
is a secondary matter, of little relevance to the common
believer. Christianity is about individual reformation, by
grace. This is his repeated message. To ignore questions
of church and society is to assume that there is already a
fixed Christian framework in which the reformed individual can participate. What I am getting at is that Lewis
is the subtlest of all defenders of Anglican establishment,
because it hardly occurs to him that it is worth defending
at all. The Church is just a natural part of life, like one's
family or the government.

Our inward transformation by grace, he boldly asserts,
'is the whole of Christianity'. A long quotation is worth-
while here, to show how his rhetorical approach and his
political assumptions interact:

> This is the whole of Christianity. There is nothing
> else. It is so easy to get muddled about that. It is
> easy to think that the Church has a lot of different
> objects – education, building, missions, holding
> services. Just as it is easy to think the State has a lot

of different objects – military, political, economic, and what not. But in a way things are much simpler than that. The State exists simply to promote and protect the ordinary happiness of human beings in this life. A husband and wife chatting over a fire, a couple of friends having a game of darts in a pub, a man reading a book in his own room or digging in his own garden – that is what the State is there for. And unless they are helping to increase and prolong and protect such moments, all the laws, parliaments, armies, courts, police, economics, etc., are simply a waste of time. In the same way the Church exists for nothing else but to draw men into Christ, to make them little Christs.[12]

Ostensibly he is offering an analogy: just as the Church exists for individual salvation, so the state exists to defend those moments of 'ordinary human happiness'. It is a notably clumsy analogy, taken at face value. Perhaps, consciously or not, Lewis is doing something rather cunning. Through an analogy, he smuggles into his definition of Christianity a vision of conservative political order. *This* is the true Church, his subtext says: an idealised England *circa* 1930; a place of pipe-smoking and potting-sheds.

Defenders of Lewis will point out that he was writing during wartime, and that 'Christian civilisation' really did seem in danger. Yet it speaks volumes that this book became a canonical text for English and American Evangelicals. Mainstream Evangelical Christianity is rooted in the contradiction of the above passage. It interprets the Gospel in terms of individual salvation. However, less openly, it identifies the Gospel with a conservative Christian social order. It will say, with great stridency, that the kingdom of God is not of this world. But it will imply all the time that the kingdom is also a certain social order, presently under threat. To be fair, this doublethink is not exclusive to Evangelicals – we have seen something similar at work in Eliot's thought.

Of course, Lewis claims to reject any culturally determined form of Christianity. He criticises the cultural Christianity that is presently in decline – this is really 'a vague theism with a strong and virile ethical code, which, far from standing over against the "world", was absorbed into the whole fabric of English institutions and sentiment and therefore demanded churchgoing as (at best) a part of loyalty and good manners and (at worst) a proof of respectability.'[13] But he is not a very convincing Kierkegaard. England's Christian culture is assumed to be synonymous with civilisation and common sense. For example, he calls monarchy a reminder of the transcendent. 'Hence a man's reaction to Monarchy is a kind of test. Monarchy can easily be "debunked"; but watch the faces, mark well the accents of the debunkers. These are the men whose tap-root in Eden has been cut: whom no rumour of the polyphony, the dance, can reach – men to whom pebbles laid in a row are more beautiful than an arch.'[14]

Lewis has an unfortunate habit of trying to win the reader's trust with wise little reflections on gender politics and the female psyche. Discussing the sin of pride, he peers into the mind of a flirtatious young woman. 'What makes a pretty girl spread misery wherever she goes by collecting admirers? Certainly not her sexual instinct: that kind of girl is quite often sexually frigid. It is Pride.'[15] Elsewhere he tries to use Freud against the feminists: 'Merely for the sake of her own erotic pleasure, to go no

further, some degree of obedience and humility seems to
be (normally) necessary on the woman's part.'[16]

I may seem to have strayed from my theme, and perhaps
in a rather grubby way. I am trying to describe Lewis'
'establishment style'; his way of associating Christianity
with cultural common sense. He often dares to give the
impression that Christians are the only people who have
an honest regard for truth; everyone else is essentially
unscrupulous, *shifty*. Christians 'are coming to be almost
the only people who appeal to the buried (but not dead)
human appetite for the objective truth.'[17] *Mere Christianity*
begins with the insistence that there is an objective Right
and Wrong. 'People may be sometimes mistaken about
them, just as people sometimes get their sums wrong,
but they are not a matter of mere taste and opinion any
more than the multiplication table.'[18] This is, alas, a lie.
Lewis did a great deal to associate Christianity with the
very intellectual dishonesty that he denounced in others.

Vidler

In 1962 a collection of essays by Cambridge theologians
was published, called *Soundings*. It inaugurated a new era
of innovative Anglican thought. Its editor, Alec Vidler,
wrote the essay dealing with the Church's relationship to
the nation. Before turning to the Church of England, he
discusses the radical thought of the wartime martyr
Dietrich Bonhoeffer, who in his last days had tried to
imagine a new form of Christianity, fit for a 'humanity
come of age' – he even used the term 'religionless Christianity'. These fragmented reflections were much discussed
in the 1960s. Vidler wonders, with Bonhoeffer, whether
religion might be able to revolutionise itself, to lose its

pervasive air of pre-modernism and meet the needs of
humanity more convincingly, more naturally.

Vidler then turns to the Church of England; he notes
that it is amazingly archaic. Its worship was last revised
in 1661; its territorial parochial system 'remains what it
has been from time immemorial'.[19] 'The form of its
relation to the state is a survival from the time when
church and commonwealth were regarded as in principle
one society', he observes. The state appoints bishops, and
'the solemn mockery of the "election" of diocesan bishops
by cathedral chapters goes on unchanged'.

> There are plenty of other archaic anomalies which
> some agitated churchmen from time to time pro-
> nounce to be 'intolerable' but which the great
> majority appear to find quite tolerable. The gener-
> ality of citizens looks upon the Church of England
> as a venerable, if curious, part of the English scene.
> They like to have it about, if only that they might
> criticise it or stay away from it. It agreeably adorns
> national and civic occasions with colourful pageantry
> and a measure of unction . . .
>
> But there is another side to the picture if we are
> considering the possible emergence of a church
> which will accept the axiom that religion is made
> for man, not man for religion. Perhaps after all this
> church is not so ill-fitted to be the seed-ground out
> of which such a church might grow. What at first
> sight look like its handicaps may prove to be its
> advantages. The very fact that no one in his senses
> can suppose the Church of England to be anything
> like the final embodiment of the kingdom of God
> or of the Christian movement in history should make

it easier for its members to acknowledge the need for radical change than it is for the members of churches that have kept more up to date as efficient organisations and so can regard their present condition as defensible and worthy of preservation.[20]

This argument is open to criticism as the epitome of Anglicanism in all its clever, well-meaning, muddled *silliness*. This Church is to be commended for being so obviously at odds with what a church ought to be! If it reformed, it might get ideas above its station, start taking itself seriously! Yet on closer inspection Vidler's case is profound. The broadness of the Church is seen not as an achievement but as a resource that resists expression; a resource that exists for the sake of some future reality. The Church is certainly a muddle, vulnerable to criticism from all sides, but within it is something unspeakably precious that we do not yet know how to extricate. (We will pursue these poetic musings in our conclusion.)

As regards the Church of England's relation to the state (the so-called 'establishment'), we have acknowledged its anomalous character, but it does not follow that it is just an archaic survival that ought forthwith to be liquidated. Sooner or later there will obviously have to be a new ecclesiastical settlement in England of some kind or other . . . Meanwhile we may well prefer to maintain the *status quo*, and to be satisfied with minor adjustments, until we are much clearer about what we want to put in its place . . . [If it were hastily disestablished], the Church of England would be cleaned up and tidied up, so that everyone could tell just what it stood

for. It is premature for any church to put itself in
that position.[21]

Of all the apologies for establishment that I here consider,
I like Vidler's the best. It reflects an awareness that Christianity is in the grip of some sort of revolution, and the
Church of England will hardly survive it intact. Vidler is
sanguine about the ending of the old order, but believes
that a slow end might be more fruitful than a quick one.
Above all he is refreshingly honest. Almost everyone else
adopts a defensive pretence that they know what is going
on. He makes room for the unknown.

After this high praise let me hasten to insist that Vidler's
defence is not in general adequate or convincing. It is
locked into the universal-service fallacy, which holds that
a true church has to be there for everyone in the country,
and that this aspiration justifies all sorts of theological
vagueness. He concludes: 'For the Church of England the
great question is whether it can be transformed into such
a church [one which meets the modern needs of the entire
nation] or is doomed to sink into the position of a religious
denomination.'[22] This is the 'bottom line' of most
defenders of establishment; we have already encountered
it a number of times. It rests on the presupposition that
a church is meant to be a pan-national society, a sort of
ghostly socialist state. This is what the Church of England
has aspired to be, such writers say, *and we must not lose
that aspiration*. Yes we must. For it is inextricable from
establishment, and from the ghost of Christendom. People
who say that the Church should withdraw from establishment as long as it retains 'the national aspiration' are
fooling themselves. It's like the rich man agreeing to
renounce his wealth, as long as he's still able to dine out

every night, and take four holidays a year. The Church must withdraw from the claim to own society.

Runcie

Runcie was not a natural rebel or reformer. He was the type to accept the structures around him, and then gently undermine them from within. He was a very Oxford intellectual — capable of being 'irreverent about everything, and serious about everything'.[23] His position on establishment was the familiar mixture of social conservatism and allegiance to as broad a Church as possible. But he was aware of the weakness of such a position, and surprisingly honest about it. In a lecture of 1981 he frankly admitted to a sort of agnosticism.

> We [as a nation] have not made up our minds whether or not to dissolve the Church/state partnership entirely and to admit that England has ceased to have a fundamentally Christian, homogenous culture or purpose and has become a geographical expression. I would not wish to hurry people into a decision one way or another: a neutral state or a Christian establishment. There is a sense in our suspicion of the doctrinaire: the attempt to impose a theoretical pattern on a confusing and diverse jigsaw of ancient institutions and modern attitudes.[24]

This is maddeningly liberal: the man is head of an established Church and still demands the right to sound non-committal. One begins to sympathise with the famous accusation that he never fails to nail his colours to the fence. Ultimately one cannot suspend decision on the establishment question in the way he seems to suggest: to stay established is to affirm a 'doctrinaire' position by default. He says that he sympathises with Anglicans impatient for disestablishment, but wonders if they fully grasp the implications.

> We ought to know what we are saying when we disclaim any wish to share further in the partnership between the Church of England and the state which has profoundly marked English society for more than a thousand years. I suspect that the divorce will be carried through, but I do not say this with any self-destructive, pseudo-apocalyptic excitement, but with a determination to make the best of present opportunities without lamenting the past or despairing for the future.[25]

The honesty, the lack of politicking, is startling. He is admitting that the institution he leads is probably incapable of being strengthened, consolidated, defended.

> It is my conviction that, although the steady progress in which the Church of England is becoming more and more an Episcopal sect cannot – and perhaps ought not to – be halted . . . it is too early to abandon altogether the vision of the Church of England as a public body, at the service of the whole nation, serving those in the outer court as well as those in the sanctuary; a Church pervasive, guarding the roots and the memories, pointing to eternity in a time of restlessness and distraction.[26]

It is 'too early to abandon' the idea of the national Church! It is hard to imagine a more restrained defence of establishment. There is a sort of tragic resignation, a holy stoicism. Establishment is on the way out, Runcie admits; but, like Vidler, he advocates letting it die as slow a death as possible. It's jolly odd that he got away with being Archbishop of Canterbury. It's like the elderly Lord Longford being minister for prisons.

Runcie was attentive to the idea we have noted in Vidler: the provisional character of this Church, and its preference of freedom to definition. 'Only a church which can comprehend diversity can believe in the developing unfolding of God's truth', he said in a sermon of 1989. 'We could make our Communion much more tidy, but it would be much less loveable, and we should be imprisoned as a result.'[27] The previous year he had told the Lambeth Conference that Anglicanism had 'a radically provisional character which we must never allow to be obscured', and it should not be 'permanently canonised'.[28]

In retirement he wondered how long establishment could last. 'I think it's going to be quite difficult for the [new] Archbishop to carry with him enough spiritual clout to be taken seriously at the centre of the nation's life. Because there is a distancing of church from state, I think. There are fewer and fewer people who are involved in making the nation tick, either politically or culturally, who have their roots in the life of the church and the Christian faith.'[29] But of course it was not in his nature to declare for disestablishment. Although establishment was doomed, the Church still needed to hold on to Nurse, 'because otherwise it's inclined to become an Episcopal sect.'[30]

Habgood

John Habgood, the former Archbishop of York, has probably been the Church's most vocal defender of establishment of the last few decades. I put him in a mental box with Richard Harries and Richard Chartres: the last old Anglicans; liberal traditionalists who vaguely believe that the Englishness of the Church will pull it through. The attitude tends to go with a fondness for cricket and (daringly) *The Goons*. A lecture that Habgood gave in 1990 provides a perfect example.

> The spirituality of the Church of England is rooted in a very English kind of consciousness. In its most typical spiritual writers there are certain easily ident-ifiable characteristics. For the most part they are moderate, practical, homely, suspicious of priestli-ness, optimistic and with not too much dwelling on the fact of sin. These may not be the greatest spiritual characteristics in the world, but they are serviceable ones. There is an order and dignity and beauty in worship. Still in most places these days there is a rootedness in English history and Catholic tradition which makes the Church both homely and uni-versal.[31]

Thirteen years on, I do not think that anyone would dare to say this sort of thing. In that change, I suppose, is the death of the Church of England. It is not so self-evident any more that this Church is stabilised by a broad middle ground of reasonable, sceptical Englishness: bluff John-sonians in the pews. In 1990 that old ideal could still be voiced; today I doubt it could be.

In 1983 he wrote a book in defence of establishment, in which the 'soul of England' argument features heavily.

> One almost inevitable consequence of disestablish-ment would be the alienation of large numbers of

people whose residual allegiance to the Church of England is bound up with the perception that in some obscure way it represents 'England'. The allegiance of many such people is already under severe strain. Religious purists would like to see them go, and would welcome disestablishment for precisely that reason. I myself believe that their departure would be a tragic loss, for them, for the church and for the nation. There, in a nutshell, is the heart of the choice.[32]

But he seems to fear for the nation most of all: nationalism might turn nasty without its religious ingredient, and 'there are reasons to be cautious . . . about supposing that disestablishment would leave the Monarchy untouched.'[33] Furthermore, the Church's own unity might be imperilled. He cites the argument that 'divisions between Catholics and Protestants, conservatives and radicals, within the Church of England are so deep that it is in effect held together only by the fact of being established. A common concern about fulfilling a national role serves to paper over the cracks.' And he hastily insists that this is 'an exaggeration, as anyone who knows the Church of England from within must surely realise.'[34] Of course.

We noted the tragic element within Runcie's reflections. Habgood is more tragic, because less stoic – he sounds like a condemned man who is not ready to die.

In an essay of 1989 he made another defence. 'The establishment gives a moral and religious identity to the nation', and is constitutionally crucial: 'I think it likely that in the absence of an Established Church the Crown could become dangerously isolated, and exposed.'[35] The idea of *danger* pervades Habgood's defence of establishment. A decade earlier he had said that our Christian heritage is at stake – 'and to dismiss this as being of no account, in my view, dangerously underestimates the extent to which our unity as a nation still depends on it.' It's almost as if the ultimate Christian duty is the defence of a conservative social order. The Tory Anglican vision is deeply ingrained even within a seemingly liberal churchman.

One of his arguments deserves more sympathy, however. 'Attempts to narrow the traditional openness of the Church of England are worrying features of today's scene . . . [T]o lose the breadth of vision and the wide tolerance which have generally been characteristic of the Established Church, would, I believe, be a great impoverishment not only to the religious lives of many individuals but also to the political life of the nation.'[36] It must be admitted that Habgood has a point: a broad, tolerant, liberal Church is preferable to sectarianism. But here is the crucial point: you cannot defend what is good (broadness) by means of defending what is indefensible (establishment).

Percy

The theologian Martyn Percy wrote an article in 1997 that responded to the rising tide of constitutional anxiety. It is fairly representative of the liberal Anglo-Catholic approach to the issue: on the one hand proud of the Church's social commitment, on the other hand critical of conservative ideology.

'The theology and ecclesiology of Anglicanism ensure that it is pro-sociality and anti-individualism', says Percy.[37] 'The Church of England is a social religion . . . Its character, identity, liturgy and practice are born out of respect for history, which includes a sense of national identity, location and community responsibility.'[38] This social commitment of Anglicanism has always been a function of its established status, he acknowledges. But now that status looks vulnerable, for various reasons: a potential crisis in the monarchy, the European Union impinging on national identity, and the imminent reform of the House of Lords. 'So far, the silence from the Church of England has been deafening. For a nationally established church, we seem to have the happy knack of losing our voices whenever the subject of "establishment" is raised.'[39]

Percy is in favour of establishment, he says, though he is 'convinced that the nature of establishment needs transforming and that the Church of England needs to push itself to the forefront of a discussion over the nature and direction of society, church, and their future relationship.'[40] As an Anglican priest he has pledged loyalty to the monarch, and he prays for her whenever he conducts the old-style service. He admits to a degree of unease about these prayers. 'The monarchy, for all its attempts at modernisation, remains caught in a time warp, shielded in a class cocoon.'[41] It is therefore hard to uphold the traditional idea that the Royal Family is representative of all families.

> The alienation of the monarchy is something that affects the Church of England deeply . . . [T]he collusion of the Church in this elitism, no matter what social good comes from it, looks an increasingly risky strategy. No one seriously sees the Queen's rule as 'ordained' by God, irrespective of what St

Paul had to say about temporal authority – the
notion simply lends a spurious divine authority to a
hegemonic *status quo*.[42]

This is a refreshingly honest admission of the crisis of
Anglican identity. But, in order to retain his faith in
establishment, Percy makes a rather perverse accusation:
the problem is caused by the monarchy's 'alienation', its
failure to modernise. When Mr Percy became a priest
and pledged loyalty to the Queen, did the Queen make
him a promise in return, that she would curb her elitism
and get in touch with her people?

He proceeds to criticise a recent shift in the Church's
self-understanding. Its emphasis upon 'mission' reflects a
culture of post-modern consumerism: it casts itself as 'an
option alongside other things or products', and resembles
a company, with 'managerial' features such as efficiency
and targets.[43] (The Turnbull Report of 1995 is charged
with conforming to such thinking.) This entails a shift
towards sharply defined membership, towards internal
clarity. But, says Percy,

> we are not called . . . to draw people away from
> society into an exclusive church. In England at least,
> and certainly in the Church of England, we affirm
> that all belong to the body unless they choose not
> to do so . . . By definition, an established church has
> no right to create or assume such a gap [between
> itself and society]; rather, it is constantly attempting
> to obviate it, knitting together heaven and earth,
> sacred and profane.[44]

The much-maligned 'woolliness' of Anglicanism serves to
prevent the domination of any interest-group or agenda –

but this is now under threat from an essentially secular ideal of institutional success.

Due to these trends, the Church is already engaged in disestablishing itself, in effect, says Percy. But this is precisely not the sort of development that Percy favours. He wants the Church to loosen, or even sever, its ties to the monarch, but to maintain, even revitalise, its commitment to all of society. The Church's establishment must undergo a sort of political enlightenment. The monarchical model is bad for the Church – it adversely affects its internal politics, as well as leading it into constitutional problems.

> I am suggesting a form of religious re-establishment, which frees the monarchy of its ties yet still obliges the Church to State and society. The heir to the throne would be free to defend faiths, marry a Roman Catholic, and/or be a Buddhist too. Following Hooker, it would still be entirely Anglican to involve the "commonwealth" of people in maintaining cathedrals, choosing deans and bishops and playing a part in the ceremonial life of the nation. A new Concordat could breathe life into the ways in which Church and State work together for the common good of all.[45]

I suspect that Percy articulates the vague yearnings of the majority of liberal Anglicans. They would love to see the removal of the monarchy problem, with all its elitist, conservative associations, and the Church's re-engagement with contemporary society. But why on earth is this likely, or even possible? Are we really to believe that the removal of the monarchy's involvement in the Church would reveal a new, democratic and vital form of establishment? Hope triumphs over realism in Percy's vision.

Scruton

Roger Scruton is a well-known exponent of English conservatism. *The Meaning of Conservatism* offers an old-fashioned Tory vision (it is therefore critical of Thatcherism). It is, of course, based on Burke's vision of the organic, hierarchical nation-state. Ideally, says Scruton, the authority of such a state will have a strong religious dimension, by means of an established church. Legal establishment is not essential: Roman Catholic Europe proves that 'there can be "establishment" even when an institution is not specifically ratified by a sovereign power'.[46] What matters is that religion upholds traditional social bonds and fosters loyalty to the corporate person of the state. The Church of England, alas, presently fails in this task, and has therefore become irrelevant: 'it has lost the principle of its politics, and therefore the allegiance of its congregation.'[47] It must repent of its liberalism and 'attend to the consoling myths of tradition.'

There is a scarcely disguised element of Hobbesian cynicism in Scruton's approach to religion; he almost admits that religion's value lies in its power of social control. He admires the religious thought of Burke and Disraeli, 'neither of whom ingenuously believed in the religion to which they both subscribed. They believed, if at all, in the self-conscious manner of the romantic, out of longing for an innocence which is lost in the process of reflecting on it.'[48] Heartbreaking.

Despite present trends, popular religion will return, he predicts:

hence the need for an established religion, and if possible an established Church. In times of disestablishment, religion fragments into fierce and muddled gestures – as among the Levellers, Ranters, Muggletonians and Seekers during the Interregnum. It is with no surprise that one should observe the spread of Manichean sects and witchcraft in America.[49]

(The refusal to engage seriously with America is characteristic of many defenders of establishment.)

Scruton's more recent book, *England: an Elegy* (2001), also relates to our theme. It is written entirely in the past tense, as if to protect Englishness from the taint of contemporary reality. The English Church, he explains, represented the core national virtues: reasonability, irony, good humour, a deep love of the local landscape and its traditions. Its form of worship was understated and dignified: 'God, as represented in the sacred text and liturgy of the Anglican Church, was an Englishman, uncomfortable in the presence of enthusiasm, reluctant to make a fuss, but trapped into making public speeches.'[50] He praises Larkin's 'Church Going', which, as we have seen, associates religious feeling with respect for what is old.

Even before the Reformation, he asserts, the Church of England had become a national religion. 'For the English, sovereignty and the national religion were ultimately identical. Hence the Reformation was imposed on them through Parliament – something that did not happen elsewhere, and which testified both to the worldliness of English religion, and to the other-worldliness of English laws.'[51] The nation did not become dogmatically Protestant: its rejection of Roman Catholicism was for political reasons. 'The true interpretation of the law of succession is not that the monarch should be a Protestant in any real sense of the term, but that he or she should be wholly and exclusively committed to upholding the law, customs and sovereignty of the English people.'[52]

For Scruton, Anglicanism is, or rather was, the happy marriage of religion and nationalist sentiment. Dogmatic Protestantism threatened this marriage in the seventeenth century: the Puritans 'were defined by their opposition from within to the gorgeous trappings of the Anglican ceremony.'[53] But their defeat cemented the marriage:

> When the frenzy and fanaticism of the seventeenth century had dwindled to a murmur, the English Church re-emerged as *Anglo-Catholic*, justified by tradition and succession, conveying unfathomable mysteries through immemorial rites. But these mysteries and rites were now bound up with England and its history, rather than with the history and ambitions of Rome. The Anglican Church had, in effect, purloined the sacraments, and used them to define local rites of passage, a local experience of membership and a national identity coterminous with 'the law of the land'.[54]

This relates to our earlier observation that the head of the Church is the monarch dressed as the pope. 'Let's face it,' Scruton has said elsewhere, 'the Church of England and the Monarchy stand or fall together, in a way . . . The Church of England is a very special thing which has, if you like, the misfortune to be attached to a particular political order and it therefore suffers the shocks of that order all the time.'[55] Misfortune? After four hundred years I'd call it careless.

Scruton's assumption is that authentic Christianity is

that which knows its place: as a loyal constituent of the Tory vision. It follows that anyone who takes religion seriously, be they Milton or Newman, is missing the point: the ideal Christian is more Machiavellian; someone like Burke, Disraeli or Churchill. Or Scruton himself, if only he could believe in it, or pretend to.

Hitchens

Peter Hitchens is the poor man's Scruton. Do not confuse him with his brother Christopher who is fiercely anti-religious. In *The Abolition of Britain* (2000), he accuses the Church of succumbing to liberal pressure in the 1960s and seeking 'relevance', through social theology and liturgical revision. Before this suicidal innovation, the Church 'was the core of the United Kingdom, Catholic *and* Reformed, open-minded yet governed by rules, intensely English, rooted in the distant past. Its version of the divine order was a mirror of the English state at the end of the seventeenth century . . . It had never been fully Catholic or Protestant, and had shrouded its beliefs in elegant vagueness.'[56]

Sadly, in the nineteenth century, 'it began a period of furious navel-gazing, disputes which mattered intensely to those involved, but baffled or repelled ordinary backsliding churchgoers as they raged on into the twentieth century and into our own time.'[57] In other words, the Church has erred in taking theology too seriously. If only it had realised that religion is about maintaining traditional social order! The Church's attempts to be relevant have failed to make it popular, and it has largely withdrawn into sectarianism. 'Almost all Anglican churches now seem to be for enthusiasts only. Few but the most determined dare enter, and many of these churches take the form of a club, unintentionally exclusive . . .'[58] The greatest loss is of the Church's liturgical universality, which allowed an Englishman to attend any church in the land and feel at home.

It is difficult to take very seriously the idea that the Church would be thriving if it had never tampered with Cranmer's prose, and never questioned traditional moral and doctrinal teaching. Yet Hitchens has a point that is not easily dismissed. Uniformity of practice was once the basis of an established Church, its rationale. To abandon the aspiration casts establishment into doubt. And it follows that an established Church's uniformity will have a national character: it will naturally foster loyalty to the nation and the monarch. He complains that in the modernisation of services, 'prayers for the Royal Family tended to get left out, but lengthy pleas about the most fashionable international crisis would be inserted.'[59] This should not be too quickly dismissed as reactionary posturing. If you want an established Church, you have to accept that it logically entails a socially conservative nationalist ideology, to ballast its unity. Strange to say, Hitchens' rabble-rousing ecclesiology is in this respect more logically consistent than that of the average bishop or theologian.

Holloway

David Holloway's book, *Church and State in the New Millennium*, is a useful, and sobering, glimpse into the conservative Evangelical mind.

If the nation does not submit to the influence of its established Church, it will descend into chaos. Does the

Church still have the right to exercise such influence? Absolutely yes, says Holloway. For there is a huge silent majority of Christians in Britain. The task, then, is to reawaken their faith, to break the spell of secularism that presently holds them. He cites research from 1994, which found that 71 per cent of the population still identify with Christianity (as we have seen, the figure from 2003 is strikingly similar: 71.7 per cent). So why does this majority fail to influence national life? He suggests that the nation's cultural life 'is being shaped by that one fifth of the population without belief.'[60] Therefore it is 'urgent that Christian citizens work for the defeat of secular humanist attitudes and policies in education, health care, social services and government – particularly those which work against the Christian faith.'[61]

He traces the triumph of secular morality back to the days of the Bloomsbury Group in the early twentieth century: 'Few outside their own circle knew about the depravity and depression that went on behind the walls of those grand terraces. It was all masked by great literary skill.'[62] Those cunning stylists! Holloway suggests that secular culture does not know what is good for it. Ironically, it even fails in its pursuit of worldly happiness. Here he cites sociological research from the US: 'The findings show that *on average* living according to God's will is beneficial.'[63] How Kierkegaard would have enjoyed this piece of intelligence! He also cites a statistic for the ladies: studies from the 1970s that show 'that religiously committed women achieve greater satisfaction in sexual intercourse with their husbands than do moderately religious or nonreligious women'.[64]

Evangelicals are keen to base their ecclesiology on the New Testament, of course. Which presents a problem in relation to the establishment question (the early Christian communities were not established). In defence of his thesis that politics should be Christian, Holloway cites Paul's admonition to Timothy, to pray 'for kings and all those in authority, that we may live peaceful and quiet lives in all godliness and holiness' (1 Timothy 2:2). He comments: 'The implications are significant. Paul was saying that politics should not only be concerned with the protection of life, limb and property (peaceful and quiet lives) but also with so structuring public life that religion (godliness) as well as morality (holiness) are helped rather than hindered.'[65] This exegesis verges on dishonesty, for it does not admit the problem of the Pauline church's non-established situation.

So what is the theological justification for establishment? 'Anglicans are committed by their history (and most Anglican Evangelicals by conviction) to what is called the "magisterial" Reformation.'[66] This means that the secular power directs the national church. But it does not mean some sort of theocracy: 'What is wanted is simply a civilisation where the majority not only admit that the Christian way of life is right and normal but also seek to shape its institutions accordingly.'[67] Is that too much to ask?

While the Christian majority allegedly exists, establishment remains valid. But he admits that the decline in Anglican allegiance is worrying. Statistics suggest 'a decline in people's self-perception as Anglican of 10 per cent every few years. In the year 2010 we could expect 10 per cent of the population to claim to be Anglican, and by the year 2020 the sense of belonging might be limited to the tiny percentage who attend regularly. That would be very serious. In no way would the Church of England then be "the Church of the nation" . . . For many

of us that would create great problems.'[68] Indeed. It would
be nice to know at what exact point these 'great problems'
for establishment would begin. Or would it still be valid
if only five per cent of the nation were Anglicans? But of
course the anomaly is not hypothetical: there are more
worshipping Roman Catholics than Anglicans in Britain.

Avis

Paul Avis is a historian of Anglicanism and a bullish
apologist for establishment. In *Church, State and Establishment*, he adopts a no-nonsense, straight-to-the-point tone.

'There is a national, as well as a local and a regional,
dimension to Christian mission', he asserts.[69] He soon
puts it more strongly: 'Like all institutions in civil society,
the churches cannot avoid being deeply involved at the
level of the state. I am afraid that those who think otherwise are deceiving themselves.'[70] Well, hang on there:
surely there are degrees of such involvement – or should
a church automatically seek to make the prince its patron?
Also there are surely some fringe churches that have no
official dealings with civil authority at all – and what
about churches that exist in hostile states? Avis protests
too much, and rather too aggressively.

'My argument does not appeal to "Englishness"
(whatever that may mean today) nor even to nationality,
and only in a muted way to any sense of national identity.
Nevertheless, given that proviso, it remains true that, in
most circumstances that are likely to arise, a faith that
persistently stands in contradiction to national identity is
in danger of being driven into a sterile sectarianism.'[71] It
is a choice, then, between cheering on national identity
and 'sterile sectarianism'. By this logic, Avis supports the

German Lutheran Church of the 1930s and the Dutch Reformed Church in South Africa during apartheid against their 'sectarian' opponents. Or are these just irrelevant exceptions to his rule?

Establishment is 'not a univocal concept', Avis warns. 'But at its lowest establishment involves some kind of recognition of a church by the state and corresponding obligations on the part of the church.'[72] In the case of the Church of England, of course, we are dealing with a high level of establishment, in which the Church's 'obligations' entail its religious incorporation of the monarch. But Avis takes this commitment for granted; he assumes that a Christian will be a monarchist. 'People who wish to remain loyal to the institution of the monarchy will be extremely cautious about calling the establishment in question. It has been recognised for centuries that the destinies of the monarchy and the church are bound up together. In our constitutional ecology, the monarchy needs the church just as the polity of the church involves the monarchy.'[73] Is 'recognised for centuries' the criterion of Christian truthfulness? At the Reformation it had been 'recognised for centuries' that the pope was indispensable. It was 'recognised for centuries' that slavery was necessary, that women should shut up in church *et cetera*. What if it is bad for the Church to be bound up with the destiny of monarchy? Or is it one's Christian duty to defend the monarchy? Note that Avis backs down, but only just, from saying, ' . . . the polity of the church *needs* the monarchy.' That would be a blasphemy.

Given his position, it is surprising that Avis dares a very brief discussion of the New Testament. Its writings 'recognise the reality of the state – in this case a pagan state – as a separate power to which the church has to relate. The New Testament's witness on this issue is not monolithic or unambiguous. The element of ambiguity in the New Testament is reflected in the subsequent history and theology of the Church.'[74] It is interesting that the text is 'ambiguous' when it fails to serve his ends. The final sentence in the above is deeply misleading: it makes out that the New Testament has essentially the same attitude to the state as subsequent Christian thought. Yet in the New Testament there are no pretensions to Christianising the state, no intentions of working in partnership with it. At best, the state is a neutral part of the created order, like the weather; at worst, as in Revelation, the state is a demonic force. Yes, God has put it there, and Christians must respect it. Must they also encourage the admixture of political authority with the Gospel of Jesus Christ? No, this would be idolatry.

Like all reactionaries, Avis emphasises that things are evolving, that nothing's set in stone. He points to the developments of the last generation, most notably the institution of General Synod. Due to these changes, 'the Church of England has, I believe, nothing to complain about in the conditions of establishment and much to be thankful for. The best approach at this juncture is surely to seize with both hands the pastoral and prophetic opportunities offered by establishment and not to fret about something that few accuse of being harmful and many recognise to be a useful service and witness.'[75] Disestablishment is the concern of immature theological minds, Avis implies, a marginal awkward squad. (Speaking entirely hypothetically, would it make any difference to Avis' case if the Archbishop of Canterbury were among the misguided few?)

There is another issue to be tackled here. Avis argues

that the practical constraints on the Church are negligible and so implies that the disestablishment case is based in mere symbolism. This is true enough: one's objection to lingering Erastianism is chiefly a matter of principle, or if you like, of symbolism. But in relation to this religion there can be no talk of *mere* symbolism. What is the rejection of idolatry but a lot of fuss over symbolism?

Avis offers us a Tory Anglican vision of Church and state in harmony.

> A national, established Church has a mission and a ministry not only to the nation as a whole and to every constituent community through the parochial structure . . . but also to people of all degrees of spiritual maturity or immaturity. It recognises pilgrims at various stages of their journey, including those who have just set out and those who have wandered from the beaten path, as its proper concern. A national, established Church, which is by definition a community church, is capacious enough to accommodate all shades of commitment. It embraces within its care those on the far reaches of the penumbra who come to church only occasionally and make contact mainly through the rites of passage as well as those who form the dedicated inner core of personnel who keep parish activities going. It leads the former back to their Christian heritage and nurtures the latter from the springs of traditional spirituality.[76]

This almost made me weep. In support of this lovely vision he refers to Gladstone's idea that the establishment brings Christianity to the 'congregated masses of misery and ignorance'. 'Gladstone's words may sound quaint and

patronising, but on reflection they are actually just as
pertinent a century and a half later.'[77] Actually no, they
are perfectly excusable coming from a great Victorian
reformer. But they sound quaint and patronising (and
worse) coming from you, today.

Bradley

In Chapter One we saw how the Coronation of 1953 was
the last gasp of the old Anglican order. Surely no theologians today condone the national cult that took place in
1953? In 2002 a theologian called Ian Bradley wrote a
book celebrating 'the spiritual dimension of monarchy'.[78]
Coronations, he explains, are valid symbols of Christian
sacrifice:

> The monarch is offered to the people, and to God,
> and dedicated to a life of selfless service and duty.
> They also involve a hallowing and consecration, a
> dedication to God of an individual and a nation,
> a setting apart and an invocation of divine blessing.
> They express particularly vividly the difficult and
> unfashionable Christian themes of vocation, disciple-
> ship and obedience . . . If we lose [coronations], or
> if we strip away too much of their symbolism and
> mystery, we take away much of the sacred signifi-
> cance of the Crown and we also lose a key moment
> of consecration and rededication in the religious
> life of the nation.[79]

Bradley writes 'to persuade fellow liberally minded and
socially committed Christians that defence of the monarchy, and active promotion of its spiritual role, should,

indeed, be part of our vocation.'[80] Perhaps I am not liberally minded enough to find his case very convincing.

'Monarchy stands at the still, stable centre of things, holding its *fir*, or truth, and keeping the forces of chaos at bay.'[81] As the archaic word suggests, Bradley is very taken with Anglo-Saxon and Celtic models. He is good proof that, in theology, there is no such thing as harmless romanticism. He believes that monarchy has a Christ-like quality: 'Christians believe that God revealed and incarnated himself in the life of a single individual. In monarchies the loyalty and aspirations of a people are focused on a single figure. It is not, I think, being idol-atrous to suggest that there is at the very least a striking parallel between the figure of Christ and that of the just and wise sovereign.'[82] One does not expect to hear such things said nowadays.

Significantly, he appeals to 'postmodern' thought to give his thesis an air of intellectual freshness. 'In contemporary Christianity there is a huge and welcome interest in symbols, in the power of the visual and the tactile, in the theology of imagination and the importance of poems and stories. Monarchy is especially rich in symbolism, visual imagery and story. Its appeal is to sentiment rather than to reason, to imagination rather than the intellect. It conforms to the Christian understanding of a sacrament as an effective sign and symbol which mediates and reveals the reality of divine grace.'[83] Bradley's theology would have gone down well in 1930s Germany, when exactly this sort of sinister Jungian trash was seen as a wonderful synthesis of traditional wisdom and modern learning.

Dr Williams' dilemma

It is time to look at the present Archbishop of Canterbury's position on establishment. As we saw in Chapter
One, when the selection of a new archbishop was
underway in 2002, Williams was assumed to be sympathetic to disestablishment. But the most frequently cited
evidence of this was circumstantial: he was Archbishop of
Wales, and the Church in Wales had been disestablished
since 1920. His actual opinion on the issue was, and is,
far from obvious.

Let us attempt a very brief overview of Williams the
social theologian. Earlier on we noted an affinity with
Michael Ramsey, another influential Anglo-Catholic theo-
logian-archbishop. In an essay of 1995, Williams reflected
on Ramsey's ecclesiology. He was sensitive to 'a perspective that was beginning to appear in continental
Catholicism and was being introduced into the ecumenical
scene largely by émigré Russian writers. It is essentially
the vision of the Church as "epiphany": what matters
about the Church is not a system of ideas as such (though
doctrine and dogma have their place) nor the structure of
an organization competent to deliver authoritative judge-
ments and to require obedience (though order is
important in its proper context), but what the bare fact
of the Church *shows* . . . Fundamentally . . . the Church
is the message.'[84]

This is a useful summary of Williams' own thought.
Every Christian principle should arise from the distinctive
practice of the Christian community. At the heart of
this distinctive practice is the Eucharist, which Williams
understands as an intrinsically political act, in its redefinition of power and community. So, instead of

communism, communionism. In an essay of 1983 the same idea is apparent: 'the orthodox Christian community identifies itself . . . by gathering to do certain things. Orthodoxy is inseparable from sacramental practice.'[85] And this practice is potentially politically radical: two years later he was arrested for singing psalms in an American air-base.

So how does this perspective see the question of establishment? Complicatedly. The ecclesiology he attributes to Ramsey (and tacitly himself) comes from Catholicism and Russian Orthodoxy, traditions that are sympathetic to establishment in one form or another. Yet once they are brought within the Anglican context, these traditions become potentially subversive of establishment: just as the Tractarians used medieval Catholic thought to criticise Erastianism. Significantly, both Ramsey and Williams come from Nonconformist backgrounds, which intensifies the shared paradox. Both are drawn to a highly Catholic ideal, but are theologically resistant to its institutional realisation, having imbibed a Protestant suspicion of Rome's claims. Both seek a balance, or synthesis, of Catholic and Protestant, and therefore value the middle way – but neither has much positive affection for establishment. It is merely a means that makes possible the holding together of theological contraries. We have seen Ramsey make this explicit, calling himself part Nonconformist, part Tractarian, but not really a C of E man. Williams would doubtless say Amen to this, in private. Indeed Williams' suspicion of Anglican establishment is surely greater than his predecessor's, for he brings a new level of political awareness to this tradition, being well versed in Marx, Nietzsche, and all their postmodern followers.

There is a strong tension in Williams' thought,

therefore, that hinges on the question of establishment. He does not often draw attention to this, but it occasionally surfaces. In an essay published in 1998, when he was Archbishop of Wales, he reflected on the Church's relationship to society. It must remain distinct from every actual society, he says, in order to witness to the universalism of the Gospel.

> [This is] more necessary than ever in a church historically prone to see itself as a national institution . . . If there is a case for the Church's establishment it must be cast in terms of the Church's witness to a community without boundaries other than Christ – not the Church's guardianship of the Christian character of a nation (which so easily becomes the Church's endorsement of the *de facto* structures and constraints of the life of a sovereign state) . . . It is doubtful whether [establishment] could speak of unrestricted human community when it will inevitably be seen as privileging one of a number of religious groupings within the state.[86]

This is a good indication of the dilemma. The conventional, conservative defence of establishment is decisively criticised, but the conclusion is not quite unequivocal. He also retains a belief that establishment has the capacity to communicate the Gospel's universality.

Two years on, he seemed to have got off the fence. In the summer of 2000, he spoke at the Greenbelt Christian music festival to a young, radical audience, and gave a surprisingly frank answer to a question about the Church's future. Establishment as it presently existed was 'not good for the Church', he said, it was a 'relic'. 'I also think that the notion of the Monarch as supreme governor has outlived its usefulness.' Establishment leads to a false sense of entitlement: 'I believe increasingly that the Church has to earn the right to be heard by the social world . . . Establishment is just one of those things that make it slightly harder.' He also said that he wanted the Church to elect its own leadership at every level, and predicted the Church would see 'disestablishment by a thousand cuts'.[87]

In 2002, when he began to be seen as a contender for Canterbury, the equivocal instinct returned. In January the *Sunday Times* quoted his comments from the Greenbelt festival a year and a half earlier. He immediately issued a press release to clarify his position:

> It seems self-evident that the disestablishment of the Church of England is something which is not going to come all at once or in the immediate future. However, with the pace of social change being what it is, this is a matter that is bound to need renego-tiation and reconsideration in the decades to come. This is something that seems to be quite widely agreed in both church and society at large . . . This is a matter which is quite clearly not at the top of the agenda for the Church of England but is climbing up the agenda.[88]

He was repositioning himself as a stoic (disestablishment is likely one day) rather than a reformer. In an interview with the *Telegraph*'s Graham Turner (unpublished until after his appointment) he made similarly conciliatory noises:

> People say that I'm in favour of disestablishment, but it is not a simple issue. There are a bundle of

legal and constitutional issues to be unpicked, but I would like to see the Crown's presence in appointments replaced by an electoral college of clergy and laity, a halving of the number of bishops in the House of Lords from the present 26 . . . It won't happen overnight but I'd want to push a little to get the appointments system changed, though not the Coronation service. The monarch going to communion is a great symbol. Ideally the phrase Supreme Governor should go, but where the shoe pinches for me is the appointments system. The message it sends out is a message of the subordination of Christianity to some kind of political interest.[89]

In question-and-answer sessions Williams seems to have a dangerous habit of saying what he thinks. Lectures can be carefully scripted to avoid blunt disclosure; off-the-cuff answers cannot. In February he spoke to the Association of Ordinands and Candidates for Ministry in Birmingham. In the discussion session he assured a questioner that disestablishment would not kill the Church, adding: 'As the philosopher Nietzsche says, "What does not kill you makes you stronger." '[90]

With the huge amount of media comment surrounding his appointment, the establishment question was swamped by others: the opposition of certain Evangelicals, and the looming war with Iraq. The news agenda moves on, and has a limited appetite for mulling over ancient theological conundrums.

In November 2002 Williams was sworn in. Soon afterwards a television profile of the new Archbishop was broadcast, in which he was mildly critical of establishment: 'It's possible to have very fruitful, very constructive relations with the government and public life without all the apparatus of legal establishment as it's evolved in England.' Also in December he gave the annual Dimbleby Lecture. Despite much postmodern circumlocution, it was a conservative thesis about the need for religion in the modern state: shades of T. S. Eliot.

In February 2003 he was enthroned. Shortly before the event he gave a couple of interviews, and the climb-down from Greenbelt radical was complete. He told the *Sunday Times* that he anticipated no retreat from the Christian character of the coronation service: 'As long as the constitutional relationship between monarch and church is there, the coronation needs to be within a Christian framework.' More widely, he affirmed the 'medieval relationship' between Church and state, though 'some of the relationships work less well than they might have 300 years ago.'[91]

A week later he gave an interview to the editor of the *Telegraph*. He was asked whether he thought 'on balance that the establishment is worth it'. Here is his full reply:

> The whole legacy which gives the Church of England a foot in the door, a way of talking this way, is a positive thing. And how that relates to the particular legal structure we are in, that is changing. I had working with me for six months in Wales some years ago an ordinand from Canada who could not believe the ease with which we got into schools. I took her with me on days when we went round six or seven schools, not church schools, and she was astonished that we were allowed to do this.[92]

That sounds like a yes, on balance. He went on to state his support for the creation of more church schools, and to remind Prince Charles that he stood to become defender of *the* faith. He did not mention his opposition to the 'supreme governor' title, or his belief in gradual disestablishment.

A sell-out? A choosing of preferment over principle? Or a cunning ruse – a Trojan Horse ploy? The truth is less dramatic, more complicated. On the issue of homosexuality he has said that he will not try to impose his liberal opinions on the Church as a whole, but to reflect majority opinion. For as archbishop he is committed to attempting to speak for all. The same is surely true on the establishment question. He has to filter out his personal opinion, for the sake of unity.

But the situation is more complicated still; it is internally complicated. I am not accusing Dr Williams of indecision on establishment, but we have noted a deep ambiguity that goes right back in his theological formation. His radical Catholicism points both ways. Like a good radical, he is deeply suspicious of the Church's role in conservative national identity; his immersion in Welsh Nonconformism confirms this. But like a good Anglo-Catholic, he believes that Christianity rightly attempts to incarnate itself in the social order, and he fears the state unloosed from its medieval spiritual moorings. For all his postmodernism, he is half in love with Christendom. (When he talks to the right-wing press he naturally allows this element of his thought to take centre stage.)

Whatever Williams' true position on establishment, one is grateful to know that he is not simply in denial, that he knows the seriousness of the issue, that he would never echo Avis' ghastly advice 'not to fret about something that few accuse of being harmful.' The few can be right, and fretting a calling.

Conclusion:

AN *ANGLICAN* POLEMIC?

L ET ME SUM UP in two sentences. The Church of
England, beneath all the modish evasion, remains
rooted in the ideal of national religious unity under the
Crown – an ideal from the sixteenth century that died
during the nineteenth century and stank during the twentieth. It is painfully clear that the Church, if it wants new
life, must cut loose from the Constantinian corpse, even
at the risk of its identity, its unity, its very existence.

Many readers will be irritated by my subtitle. If I admit
that disestablishment will end the Church of England as we
know it, how dare I lay claim to the adjective 'Anglican' at
all?

Some will see my response as paradoxical, disingenuous
and even rather barmy. Others will sense the first fresh
words on this tradition in many decades. As we have seen,
this Church has claimed to encompass both Catholic and
Protestant elements, to have the best of both worlds.
According to my argument, this claim is unsustainable.
For the coexistence of Catholic and Protestant has always
depended on the unifying force of the national ideal.
When this crumbles (which is now), the Church is extra-
ordinarily weak and disunited: a sinking ship.

So surely I ought to jump this sinking ship and nail my

colours to another mast? But no: *here* I stand. Anglicanism
is the best-positioned form of Christianity in existence,
despite its unsustainability. It is dying but it points the
way, like Moses before the promised land.

Let us restate why: it has held together the principles
of Catholicism and Protestantism. This holding together
is a boldly *critical* act. Each ecclesial model is placed in
judgement by the presence of the other. In this tradition,
when it is healthy, both Catholic and Protestant traditions
are forced to confront their own shortcomings. But how
can this co-existence avoid being a warm mush of
compromise that satisfies none and signifies nothing?

Anglicanism's straddling of Catholic and Protestant
must be re-read, seen from the opposite perspective. The
via media must be turned inside-out. As well as being
implicated in both traditions, Anglicanism also has a
unique freedom from both. It is sceptical about both of
the major accounts of Christian identity. And I believe
that such scepticism is entirely warranted: we need a
revolution in Christian identity that is beyond the imagination of any existing church. Yet Anglicanism is in a
better position than most, due to its incredible theological
freedom. Other churches are more theologically, ecclesi-
ologically fixed. This makes them stronger in the short
run, but less able to change, and to point ahead. Anglicanism has the jewel of infinite price: ecclesiological
freedom. This freedom was bought by means of establishment, I know, but it must now be wrested free of it. We
must loot the Egyptians.

Anglicanism is the failure of historical Christianity
incarnate. It is where that failure is forced to know itself,
it is where talk of 'reform' becomes merely ironic. It is
the twilight of the churches. So why should it not

become the cockpit of the coming revolution in Christian identity? We recall Vidler's tentative suggestion that the slow and awkward demise of Anglicanism might in fact be very far from pointless, that there might even be something here for Bonhoeffer, and his vision of some sort of *uber*-church: 'Perhaps after all this church is not so ill-fitted to be the seed-ground out of which such a church might grow.'[1] In a similar vein, the theologian David Edwards recently offered some advice to Dr Williams: 'The vision of Michael Ramsey needs to be revived: the vocation of Anglicanism (which is not a systematic *ism*) is to point to the Church in which all the denominations (or all the historic ones) will have "died" in order to rise.'[2] Maybe it is time for this vision of Anglicanism to emerge into the daylight; blinking and stumbling at first, no doubt. The imminent demise of establishment is its historic chance.

I know it sounds rather predictable to coin a label, but anyone for Post-Anglicanism? Post-Anglicans are those who know that their Church is dying, but believe that its death will give life to Christianity, in crazy abundance. Outwardly, Post-Anglicans resemble old-fashioned Anglicans, in touch with both Catholic and Protestant traditions, which means critical of both. But a crucial inner shift has occurred. What Post-Anglicans celebrate is not positive – the union of Catholic and Protestant, but *negative* – their freedom from both. For no existing account of the Church impresses them entirely. The two basic models are radically flawed, both Catholic and Reformed. The normal Anglican approach is to be desperately polite about each side. But Post-Anglicans realise that it is our criticism of each that matters, and that it is too late in the day to fear giving offence. The initial problem for Post-Anglicans is that theology is presently ruled by pedantry and politeness: we must learn to speak straight.

And so we must openly say that the dominant Catholic account of authority smells of violence, and leads to a pre-modern, legalistic ecclesiology. And we must openly say that the dominant Protestant account of faith is infantile, and leads to a pre-modern, legalistic ecclesiology. We do not like the idea of the Church as a magic society, to be within which is to be saved; and we do not like the idea of the Church as the congregation of the individually saved. (Our argument is obviously with both accounts of salvation as well as both accounts of Church.)

The traditional Anglican solution is a compromise between two flawed models of Church, held together by a desperately outmoded political ideology. Post-Anglicanism turns this round: the *via media* is not the solution, but the space in which the new will emerge. How? In the first instance by a clear-eyed, pan-critical appraisal of contemporary Christian identity. But Post-Anglicanism does not rush in to mend the unmendable. It sits tight, secretly plotting a daring and messy operation: ripping the heart out of Anglicanism, in order to donate it to the Christian future. But it does not rush into this either. Post-Anglicanism is characterised by cunning and reserve. It holds itself back, watchful, poised, like a tightened bow. And waits, amazed.

Notes

❧

Introduction

1. *London Link* (Diocese of London newspaper), Easter 2003, p. 3.

1. Undead: Establishment Since 1953

1. Adrian Hastings, *A History of English Christianity 1920–2000* (SCM, 2001), p. xv.
2. Ben Pimlott, *The Queen: Elizabeth II and the Monarchy* (HarperCollins, 2001), p. 194.
3. Ibid., p. 209.
4. Paul A. Welsby, *A History of the Church of England 1945–1980* (Oxford University Press, 1984), p. 9.
5. Hastings 2001, pp. 436–7.
6. Pimlott 2001, p. 210.
7. Ibid., p. 213.
8. Hastings 2001, p. 425.
9. Ibid., p. 427.
10. Welsby 1984, p. 44.
11. George Orwell, *Collected Essays, Journalism and Letters, Vol. 3* (Penguin, 1968), p. 21.
12. Stephen Sykes, 'The Genius of Anglicanism', in *The English Religious Tradition and the Genius of Anglicanism*, ed. by Geoffrey Rowell (IKON, 1992), p. 234.
13. Michael Saward, *A Faint Streak of Humility, an Autobiography* (Paternoster, 1999), p. 140.
14. Peter Hitchens, *The Abolition of Britain: The British Cultural Revolution from Lady Chatterley to Tony Blair* (Quartet, 2000), p. 110.
15. Clifford Longley, *Chosen People: the Big Idea that Shapes England and America* (Hodder & Stoughton, 2002), p. 268.
16. Hastings 2001, p. 664.
17. Welsby 1984, pp. 75–6.
18. Ibid., p. 228.
19. Ibid., p. 50.

20. Ibid., p. 52.
21. Michael Ramsey, quoted in Welsby 1984, p. 109.
22. Hastings 2001, p. 651.
23. Callum Brown, *The Death of Christian Britain* (Routledge, 2001), p. 1.
24. Ibid., p. 8.
25. Hastings 2001, p. 606.
26. Welsby 1984, p. 193.
27. Ibid., p. 603.
28. Ibid., p. 615.
29. David Martin, 'Personal Identity and a Changed Church', in *No Alternative, the Prayer Book Controversy*, ed. by David Martin and Peter Mullen (Blackwell, 1981), p. 22.
30. Hastings 2001, p. 608.
31. A. N. Wilson, in *Why I am Still an Anglican*, ed. by Toby Churton (Collins, 1986), pp. 37–8.
32. Alan Bennett, 'Comfortable Words', in *Writing Home* (Faber, 1997), p. 541.
33. Ibid., p. 542.
34. Beryl Bainbridge, 'When Prayer Goes Pop', in *No Alternative, the Prayer Book Controversy*, ed. by David Martin and Peter Mullen (Blackwell, 1981), pp. 136–7.
35. Fay Weldon, 'A Church Bent on Self-Destruction: a View from a Newcomer', in *Called to Account: the Case for an Audit of the State of the Failing Church of England*, ed. by Digby Anderson and Peter Mullen (The Social Affairs Unit, 2003), p. 58.
36. Martin Amis, 'The Voice of the Lonely Crowd', *Guardian*, 1 June 2002.
37. Arnold Hunt, 'In Search of the Anglican', *TLS*, 21 December 2001.
38. George Carey, *I Believe* (SCM, 1990), p. 175.
39. Ibid., p. 191.
40. Peter Clarke, *Hope and Glory, Britain 1900–1990* (Penguin, 1997), p. 161.
41. Hitchens 2000, p. 120.
42. Nicky Gumbel, *Questions of Life, an Opportunity to Explore the Meaning of Life* (Hodder & Stoughton, 2001), p. 203.
43. Ibid., p. 204.
44. Robert Van de Weyer, *Dear Rowan* (John Hunt, 2002), p. 65.
45. Ibid., p. 34.

46. Carey 1990, p. 197.

47. William Oddie, *The Roman Option: Crisis and the Realignment of English Speaking Christianity* (HarperCollins, 1997), p. 45.

48. Ibid., p. 56.

49. Stephen Sykes, 'The Genius of Anglicanism', in *The English Religious Tradition and the Genius of Anglicanism*, ed. by Geoffrey Rowell (IKON, 1992), p. 230.

50. Pimlott 2001, p. 480.

51. Ken Leech, *Guardian*, 9 January 1993.

52. John Habgood, *The Times*, 30 January 1993.

53. Colin Buchanan, *Cut the Connection, Disestablishment and the Church of England* (SPCK, 1994), p. 59.

54. Ibid., p. 70.

55. Ibid., p. 73.

56. Ian Bradley, *God Save the Queen, The Spiritual Dimension of Monarchy* (Darton, Longman & Todd, 2002), p. 165.

57. Ibid., p. 153.

58. *Independent on Sunday*, 17 January 1999.

59. Libby Purves, 'Keep Church and State Apart', *The Times*, 9 October 2001.

60. Clifford Longley, 'A Bond Anglicans Must Break', *The Tablet*, 19 January 2002.

61. Hywel Williams, 'We Must Set Those Poor Bishops Free', *Guardian*, 8 January 2002.

62. George Carey, reported in *The Times*, 24 April 2002.

63. Michael Turnbull, 'The Woman Who Will Name the Next Archbishop of Canterbury', *Telegraph*, 27 March 2002.

64. *Church Times*, 12 July 2002.

65. Colin Buchanan, 'Keep Downing Street Away from Canterbury', *The Tablet*, 29 July 2002.

2. Hooker's Ghost: the Anglican Centuries

1. Diarmaid MacCulloch, *Thomas Cranmer* (Yale, 1996), p. 55.

2. Anthony Kenny, *Thomas More* (Oxford University Press, 1983), p. 87.

3. Ibid., p. 278.

4. Ibid., p. 279.

5. Ibid.

6. Ibid., p. 577.

7. William Temple, quoted in Adrian Hastings, *A History of English Christianity 1920–2000* (SCM, 2001), p. 49.

8. Adrian Hastings, 'episcopate' entry in *The Oxford Companion to Christian Thought*, ed. by Adrian Hastings, Alistair Mason and Hugh Pyper (Oxford University Press, 2000), p. 204.

9. William Haller, *The Rise of Puritanism* (Harper & Row, 1957), p. 343.

10. A. N. Wilson, *The Victorians* (Hutchinson, 2002), p. 586.

11. Alec Vidler, *The Church in an Age of Revolution* (Penguin, 1967), p. 34.

12. Ibid., p. 81.

13. Samuel Taylor Coleridge, *On the Constitution of Church and State*, ed. by John Barrell (Dent, 1972), p. 53.

14. Ibid., p. 59.

15. Vidler 1967, p. 45.

16. Paul Avis, *Anglicanism and the Christian Church* (Continuum, 2002), p. 165.

17. John Keble, in David Nicholls (ed.), *Church and State in Britain Since 1830* (SPCK, 1967), p. 154.

18. Avis 2002, p. 261.

19. John Henry Newman, *Apologia Pro Vita Sua* (Collins, 1959), p. 123.

20. Nicholls 1967, p. 49.

21. Newman 1959, p. 137.

22. Avis 2002, p. 302.

23. Ibid., p. 201.

24. W. E. Gladstone, *The State in its Relations to the Church*, quoted in Avis 2002, p. 178.

25. W. E. Gladstone, letter to Manning, 5 April 1835, in Nicholls 1967, pp. 57–8. L26.

26. Philip Magnus, *Gladstone* (John Murray, 1963), p. 189.

27. George Eliot, *Scenes of Clerical Life* (Penguin, 1998), p. 257.

28. Ibid., pp. 264–5.

29. P. T. Forsyth, quoted in Clyde Binfield, 'P. T. Forsyth as Congregational Minister', in *Justice the True and Only Mercy, Essays on the Life and Theology of Peter Taylor Forsyth*, ed. by Trevor Hart (T. & T. Clark, 1995), p. 194.

30. Hastings 2001, pp. 112–13.

31. Ibid., p. 54.

32. Clifford Longley, *Chosen People: the Big Idea that Shapes England and America* (Hodder & Stoughton, 2002), p. 205.

33. Ibid., p. 209.

34. Peter Hitchens, *The Abolition of Britain: The British Cultural Revolution from Lady Chatterley to Tony Blair* (Quartet, 2000), p. 43.

35. William Temple, letter to *The Times*, 28 June 1917, in John Kent, *William Temple: Church, State and Society in Britain 1880–1950* (Cambridge University Press, 1992), p. 77.

36. Ibid., p. 78.

37. Ibid., p. 33.

38. Ibid., p. 35.

39. Owen Chadwick, *Hensley Henson, a Study in the Friction between Church and State* (Oxford University Press, 1983), p. 207.

40. Owen Chadwick, *Michael Ramsey, a Life* (Clarendon, 1990), p. 190.

3. Recent Apologists

1. T. S. Eliot, *After Strange Gods* (Faber & Faber, 1933), p. 57.

2. Ibid., p. 19.

3. T. S. Eliot, *The Idea of a Christian Society* (Faber & Faber, 1939), p. 63.

4. Ibid., pp. 29–30.

5. Ibid., p. 46.

6. Ibid., p. 49.

7. Ibid., p. 50.

8. Ibid., p. 54.

9. Ibid., p. 58.

10. C. S. Lewis, *Mere Christianity* (HarperCollins, 1997), p. vi.

11. Ibid., p. 33.

12. Ibid., p. 164.

13. C. S. Lewis, *God in the Dock* (W. B. Eerdmans, 1970), p. 219.

14. C. S. Lewis, 'Equality', in *Present Concerns, Ethical Essays* (Fount, 1986), p. 20.

15. Lewis 1997, p. 102.

16. Lewis 1986, p. 19.

17. Ibid., p. 66.

18. Lewis 1997, p. 3.

19. Alec Vidler, 'Religion and the National Church', in *Soundings, Essays Concerning Christian Understanding*, ed. by A. R. Vidler (Cambridge University Press, 1962), p. 257.

20. Ibid.

21. Ibid., p. 261.
22. Ibid.
23. Humphrey Carpenter, *Robert Runcie, the Reluctant Archbishop* (Hodder & Stoughton, 1996), p. 106.
24. Robert Runcie, *Windows onto God* (SPCK, 1983), p. 65.
25. Ibid., p. 67.
26. Ibid., p. 73.
27. Sermon delivered in Kerala, 1989, quoted in Mary Tanner, ' "I'm Robert, What's your Name?": Runcie and the Anglican Communion', in *Runcie: On Reflection: An Archbishop Remembered*, ed. by Stephen Platten (Canterbury Press, 2002), pp. 79–80.
28. Ibid., p. 73.
29. Carpenter 1996, p. 371.
30. Ibid., p. 129.
31. John Habgood, *Making Sense* (SPCK, 1993), pp. 179–80.
32. John Habgood, *Church and Nation in a Secular Age* (SPCK, 1983), p. 109.
33. Ibid.
34. Ibid., p. 110.
35. Habgood 1993, p. 148.
36. Ibid.
37. Martyn Percy, 'The State of the Church We're In', *Affirming Catholicism*, Journal no. 23, Winter–Spring 1997, p. 5.
38. Ibid.
39. Ibid.
40. Ibid., p. 6.
41. Ibid.
42. Ibid.
43. Ibid., p. 9.
44. Ibid., pp. 9–10.
45. Ibid., p. 14.
46. Roger Scruton, *The Meaning of Conservatism*, 3rd edn (Palgrave, 2001; 1st edn 1980), p. 160.
47. Ibid., p. 161.
48. Ibid., p. 157.
49. Ibid., p. 162.
50. Roger Scruton, *England: an Elegy* (Pimlico, 2001), p. 91.
51. Ibid., p. 98.
52. Ibid., p. 103.
53. Ibid., p. 104.

54. Ibid., pp. 110–11.

55. 'Right out of Fashion', interview with Luke Bretherton, in *Third Way*, April 2001.

56. Peter Hitchens, *The Abolition of Britain: The British Cultural Revolution from Lady Chatterley to Tony Blair* (Quartet, 2000), p. 115.

57. Ibid., pp. 116–17.

58. Ibid., p. 124.

59. Ibid., p. 128.

60. David Holloway, *Church and State in the New Millennium* (HarperCollins, 2000), p. 42.

61. Ibid., p. 11.

62. Ibid., p. 44.

63. Ibid., p. 6.

64. Ibid., p. 164.

65. Ibid., p. 41.

66. Ibid., p. 219.

67. Ibid., p. 217.

68. Ibid., p. 219.

69. Paul Avis, *Church, State and Establishment* (SPCK, 2001), p. viii.

70. Ibid., p. x.

71. Ibid., p. 15.

72. Ibid., p. 21.

73. Ibid., p. 31.

74. Ibid., p. 39.

75. Ibid., p. 34.

76. Ibid., pp. 81–2.

77. Ibid., p. 82.

78. Ian Bradley, *God Save the Queen, The Spiritual Dimension of Monarchy* (Darton, Longman & Todd, 2002).

79. Ibid., p. 93.

80. Ibid., p. x.

81. Ibid., p. 201.

82. Ibid., p. 202.

83. Ibid., p. 204.

84. Rowan Williams, 'Theology and the Churches', in *Michael Ramsey as Theologian*, ed. by Robin Gill and Lorna Kendall (Cowley Publications, 1995), pp. 13–14.

85. Rowan Williams, 'What is Catholic Orthodoxy?' in *Essays Catholic and Radical*, ed. by Ken Leech and Rowan Williams (Bowerdean Press, 1983), pp. 13–14.

86. 'Incarnation and the Renewal of Community', in Rowan Williams, *On Christian Theology* (Blackwell, 2000), pp. 233–4.

87. *The Sunday Times*, 27 January 2002.

88. Press release, the Church in Wales, 27 January 2002.

89. Graham Turner, 'Thoughts on the road to Canterbury' (reporting an interview with Williams at an unspecified date 'earlier this year'), *Telegraph*, 24 July 2002.

90. *Church Times*, 8 February 2002.

91. Interview with Christopher Morgan, *The Sunday Times*, 2 February 2003.

92. Interview with Charles Moore, *Telegraph*, 12 February 2003.

Conclusion: an *Anglican* Polemic?

1. Alec Vidler, 'Religion and the National Church', in *Soundings, Essays Concerning Christian Understanding*, ed. by A. R. Vidler (Cambridge University Press, 1962), p. 257.

2. David Edwards, 'A Master Mariner Meets the Storm', *The Tablet*, 27 July 2002.

Index